William Hamilton Burns (1779–1859)

ed from a calotype photograph by D. O. Hill and R. Adamson

: National Galleries of Scotland. Elliot Collection, bequeathed 1950.
Used by Permission.

THE PASTOR O

Reprodu

Ima

THE
PASTOR OF
KILSYTH

OR,

MEMORIALS

OF THE

LIFE AND TIMES OF THE REV. W. H. BURNS D.D.

BY THE REV. ISLAY BURNS

ST. PETER'S FREE CHURCH, DUNDEE

THE BANNER OF TRUTH TRUST

THE BANNER OF TRUTH TRUST

Head Office
3 Murrayfield Road
Edinburgh
EH12 6EL
UK

North America Office
PO Box 621
Carlisle
PA 17013
USA

banneroftruth.org

First published 1860
This edition © The Banner of Truth Trust 2019
Reprinted 2020 (twice)

*

ISBN
Print: 978 1 84871 871 5
EPUB: 978 1 84871 872 2
Kindle: 978 1 84871 873 9

*

Typeset in 11/14 Adobe Garamond Pro
at The Banner of Truth Trust, Edinburgh

Printed in the USA by
Versa Press Inc.,
East Peoria, IL.

N.B. Footnotes placed in square brackets in this
edition have been added by the publisher.

CONTENTS

PUBLISHER'S INTRODUCTION

T*HE Pastor of Kilsyth* introduces us to the life and ministry of William Hamilton Burns (1779–1859), the father of the better known preacher and missionary to China William Chalmers Burns (1815–68). But while eclipsed in fame by his son, the life and ministry of William H. Burns contains much that is of value to us today. This is reflected by Iain Murray who referred to *The Pastor of Kilsyth* as a "little known work," but notwithstanding this said it is "one of the best Scottish ministerial biographies."[1] Those who give time to read this book will undoubtedly be led to agree with Murray.

The author of *The Pastor of Kilsyth* was another son of William H. Burns, Islay Burns (best known as a writer, and as the successor to Robert Murray M'Cheyne in Dundee). He gave three reasons for writing this biography, and they are still helpful in outlining its value. Islay

---

[1] Iain H. Murray, *A Scottish Christian Heritage* (Edinburgh: Banner of Truth, 2006), 121.

Burns first said that he aimed to introduce his readers to a "humble, unobtrusive, loving, cheerfully serious, and quietly conscientious country clergyman." What we have here then is the life of an "ordinary" faithful pastor. He held no prestigious pulpit, he held no important professorship in theology. He founded no institution. He simply laboured in relative obscurity, but did so faithfully and with perseverance. Yes, he ultimately saw great revival. But along the way there were spiritually discouraging days in the nation, there was personal hardship (for example, the early death of children) and sacrifice (for example, in supporting the founding of the Free Church of Scotland he gave up his manse and church building) and years of no great visible fruit.

In our celebrity-driven age (from which the evangelical church is far from exempt), this is exactly the kind of life we need to study. We need to be reminded of the beauty, dignity and ultimately the glory of humble, obscure Christian service (Matt. 10:42). Yes, we need the towering leaders of men like John Calvin and John Knox. However, the great work of the church is ultimately carried forward by those who receive little earthly reward and recognition (but great is their reward in heaven!). William H. Burns was one of these, and we need many like him in our day. We need those whose life can be summarized thus: "He preached the word; dispensed the sacred supper; warned the careless; comforted the sorrowing; baptized little children; blessed the union of young and loving hearts; visited the sick, the dying; buried the dead; pressed the hand, and whispered words of peace into the ear of mourners; carried to the poor widow and friendless orphan the charity of the church and his own; slipt in softly into some happy home and gently broke the sad news of the sudden disaster far away; lifted up the fallen one from the ground, and pointed to Him who receiveth the publicans and the sinners … [He was] always at his work, and always happy in it, and desiring nothing better or higher on earth."

The second reason this biography was written was to "preserve the fast-fading lineaments of an age, and of a race of worthies, of which the Pastor of Kilsyth had become the almost sole surviving representative." Islay Burns here hints at something of the distinctive piety that characterized William H. Burns and many of his generation. To be sure they had their faults, perhaps the most obvious being drawing sharp lines of demarcation between godly and ungodly activities without express scriptural warrant (today, we have overreacted with the opposite error). But taken all in, Burns, and others like him, introduce us to a kind and type of piety which reveals the genuine power of godliness (2 Tim. 3:5). Like the memoirs of Thomas Boston,[1] the life of Burns introduces us to "another world" in the best sense of the phrase. To read the *Pastor of Kilsyth* is to be in

---

[1] Thomas Boston, *Memoirs of Thomas Boston* (Edinburgh: Banner of Truth, 1988).

the presence of one who "walked with God." Burns's life calls us to live on a higher spiritual plane, to live more Christ shaped lives.

The third reason this book was written was to "give reply … to inquiries … made concerning the validity and the permanence of a remarkable work of grace." And this introduces us to the wonderful revival that occurred in Burns's parish of Kilsyth in 1839. Burns has longed for revival for many years prior to 1839, and had not neglected the ordinary means of grace in his desire for a greater blessing. Indeed, "it was not by any grand *coup de main*, or by a series of fitful, brilliant charges, that he expected to produce great results; but by a patient course of holy duty, continued on in faith and prayer from year to year." But how stirring it is to read of the great movement of the Spirit in the 1839 revival in Kilsyth! To be reminded that when God so pleases, he can in a moment transfer multitudes from death to life is surely to call us up to desire these things in our day!

The theological reflections of Burns on revival (as well as examples of his sermons) contained in *The Pastor of Kilsyth* are particularly helpful. In considering the factors which he believed important in connection with the revival Burns highlighted four things. First, prayer, both corporate and private. Second, the use of extra means beyond the usual preaching of the gospel in the church to reach out to the wider community. Third, a support for overseas mission, as a concern for conversions in one part of the world is naturally connected to a desire for conversions in other parts. Fourth, bringing a Christian influence into the "weaver's shops," *i.e.* those places in society where conversations about important topics take place. All of these four areas are directly applicable today.

Well, these three reasons are enough to justify the reprinting of *The Pastor of Kilsyth.* However, we should not, of course, seek to slavishly imitate the pattern of ministry William H. Burns had. We belong to a different age, and we are called to serve God in our generation. The ministries of today must of necessity have the stamp of the twenty-first century on them. But with respect to the substance of his character, and the essence of his ministry we would all do well to imitate the Pastor of Kilsyth. The piety he modelled, the faithfulness of his ministry, his confidence in the work of the Spirit through the preached word. If these, and other traits of his life, were more evident today, it would be to the great good of the church. As Islay Burns wrote, "With the departure of the form may some portion, at least, of the old spirit still remain with us!"

DONALD JOHN MACLEAN
Elder, Cambridge Presbyterian Church
Trustee, Banner of Truth Trust
February 2019

The Manse, Kilsyth (from the original edition of 1860).

PREFACE

MY aim in the following pages, besides the immediate purpose of rearing a modest, but meet memorial of one whose eminent worth and usefulness had made his name to an unusual extent known and fragrant throughout the land, has been chiefly threefold:—

First, I have endeavoured to sketch, at least, in a few distinct and truthful lines, the image of the life and the ways of a class of men of whom our subject was a singularly winning and characteristic specimen,—that of the humble, unobtrusive, loving, cheerfully serious, and quietly conscientious country clergyman, something between George Herbert's "Parson" and Richard Baxter's "Pastor," to whom, albeit unknown, perhaps even by name, beyond the limits of their own immediate sphere, the Church and the country alike owe so much, as the unseen feeders of their deepest springs of life and health.

Secondly, I have sought to preserve the fast-fading lineaments of an age, and of a race of worthies, of which the Pastor of Kilsyth had become the almost sole surviving representative, and of whose memories his rich store of personal reminiscence made him as it were the custodier and depositary. The work thus partakes somewhat of the historical as well as of the biographical character,—aiming not so much to fix the attention of its readers on one single portrait, as to lead them along the shady gallery in which may be seen, at least in faint outline, the visages of many other faithful witnesses of a dark day,—most of whom, though burning and shining lights in their time, have received no other memorial on earth.

Finally, I have been specially anxious to give reply, brief, but I trust distinct and sufficient, to inquiries now so often made concerning the validity and the permanence of a remarkable work of grace, on which, after the lapse of twenty years, the events of the present hour are casting the light of a fresh interest and importance.

The materials I have employed, besides my own personal recollections and those of other friends, have been certain copious memoranda of the events and the men of his time, written at the suggestion of clerical friends by my father himself, some years before his death, together with a brief record of daily occurrences begun in 1808, and continued to the close of his life.

The few "Remains" at the close have been selected from amid the vast accumulated stores of sixty years, simply with a view to their illustrative bearing on the incidents of the preceding narrative, with the exception only of the last, which is given as a good specimen of the author's usual style of preaching.

The Vignette will be recognised by many who visited Kilsyth during the solemn scenes of 1839, as taken from the rising ground to the south of the manse, now slightly altered, which was then his home, and which formed the centre of the most interesting and important events in his life.

ISLAY BURNS
DUNDEE
April 30, 1860

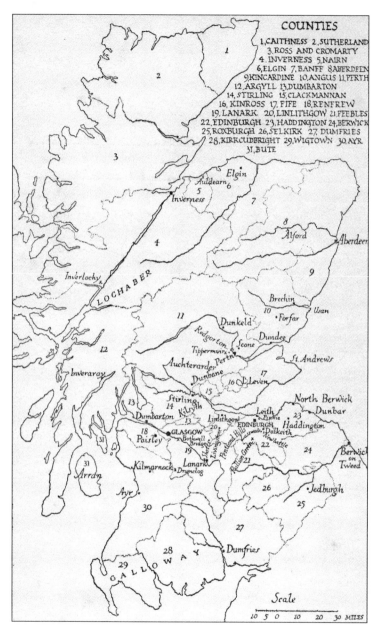

Map of Scotland.

CHAPTER I

1779–1791

BIRTH AND CHILDHOOD

———

From a child thou hast known the holy scriptures, which are able to make thee wise unto salvation through faith which is in Christ Jesus.—2 Tim. iii. 15.

STRONG and reasonable as is the desire to know all the circumstances connected with the birth and early years of those whose life has been in any way memorable or specially interesting to us, it is but seldom that that desire can be fully gratified. The early years in the life of a man, like the early ages in the life of a nation, are for the most part buried in obscurity. Like the sources of mighty rivers, the first springs of human existence and of human history lie far up among the everlasting hills, and are shrouded in mist and cloud.

The period of childhood and early youth is long passed, before it can be known that there is to be anything in the character and career of the individual in question deserving to be singled out from the herd as the object of special commemoration; and by that time the materials for a full biography of early years no longer exist. The only person that now survives qualified in any degree to supply the blank is probably the subject of inquiry himself; and then, while truly noble natures are perhaps the least disposed to furnish such details in regard to themselves, the faint and shadowy memories of childish days would scarcely enable them to do so if they would. The most remarkable records of wise and holy childhood are doubtless those which embalm the memory of those fair flowers which have been transplanted in their very first blossom from earth to heaven, and whose early removal has led to the quick gathering together and treasuring up of precious fragments that had otherwise been for ever lost. Of those who remain to riper years there are probably many whose childish words and ways were equally worthy of remembrance, were there the same motive for recording them; but the man survives to supersede the child, and those early ripple marks of life are effaced and swept away by the stronger tides of after years. So, that best of all books of holiest wisdom and truth (second only to the Eternal Word itself)—the face and the heart of a child—is consigned ever to fading parchments, and must be read in ever fresh editions in each successive generation, even in that particular "little one," whom the great Teacher for the time being places in the midst of us. It is remarkable that in the greatest of all biographies the first three decades of life are almost an entire blank. The holy child of Nazareth grew up to manhood in a mysterious secrecy and silence, unbroken save by a single incident, that of his visit to the temple in his twelfth year,—"that solitary floweret gathered from the enclosed garden of the thirty years." Even in such a case as that of Samuel, where the interest of the biography so largely turns upon the incidents of birth and early years, we scarcely know much more. That he was the child of many prayers, of early dedication to God, of godly and careful up-bringing,—this much we know,—but little more, until the time when the final decisive call of God summoned him from the quiet precincts of the sanctuary, where his young life had been silently unfolding into the arena and stern struggle of public action. The subject of the present brief memorial is no exception to this rule. There is no trace in any family records or reminiscences of anything remarkable and specially memorable in his childhood and early youth. All we certainly know is, that he, like Samuel, was the child of godly and honourable parentage, and like him, planted by a parent's hand in the house of God, and watered, there is reason to believe from the first not in vain, by a parent's prayers. His father, Mr. John Burns, officer of the customs at Borrowstownness, and latterly factor for the Duke of Hamilton on the Kinneal estate, was a fine specimen of that sober, solid, fervent, and truly patriarchal piety, of which the Scottish nation and Scottish Church are happily so rich, and which constitute the true glory and strength of our land. He was blessed, by his first and only wife, Grizzel Ferrier,[1] a true helpmeet, with twelve children, of whom ten, eight sons and two daughters,[2] lived to occupy positions of respectability and usefulness in the world. He was borne to the grave at the ripe age of eighty-six, by his eight sons, of whom no fewer than seven belonged to the learned professions, three as lawyers, and four parochial ministers of the Church of Scotland. Of this goodly group the subject of this sketch was the fifth, and was born on the 15th of February 1779. In the genial atmosphere of that godly home, there is reason to believe that the germs of saving grace were early sown in his heart, and gradually ripened into a gentle and loving piety, which grew with his growth, and strengthened with his strength. Besides the parental influence, another gracious element was early infused into the family life, in the example and spirit of his oldest brother, the Rev. James Burns, late minister of Brechin, who may be truly said, like the Baptist, to have been sanctified by the Spirit from his mother's

[1] Daughter of John Ferrier, Esq., writer, Linlithgow, and Grizzel, daughter and heiress of Sir Walter Hamilton, Bart., of Westport, Linlithgowshire.

[2] Mrs. David Guthrie, sen., Brechin, and Mrs. Professor Briggs, St. Andrews, both still alive.

womb, and consecrated by the first and strongest bias of his heart to the service of God. As if destined from the first to minister before the Lord in the priest's office, he was a preacher even from a child, and that apparently not altogether from mere childish imitation, but out of a real love for God's house and service. To gratify as well as foster this early choice, the highest and the holiest in the eyes of a godly Scottish parent of his class and age, his kind father was at the expense of erecting a domestic pulpit, from which his young Levite might exercise his gifts in a friendly congregation of servants and neighbours, and which, after serving the uses of its first occupant, descended in succession to other members of the family who were in turn smitten with the ambition to follow his steps. It may be mentioned as an interesting circumstance, that the youngest of the family, and the last who studied for the holy ministry, the Rev. George Burns, D.D., of Corstorphine, was himself baptized from the same pulpit by the then venerable minister of the parish, who conducted divine service in it on the occasion. This venerable heirloom became ultimately the property of the subject of this sketch, who preserved it for many years at the manse of Kilsyth as a sacred relic of former days, to be called into active service again, as we shall hereafter see, for yet higher work, and amid more earnest and stirring scenes.

My father's earliest memories connected at all with religious matters date from his ninth year (anno 1788), and have reference to a solemn day of public thanks-giving for the blessings of the "glorious revolution," accomplished a hundred years before. He remembered distinctly having been present in the church of Borrow-stownness on that occasion; and the faces and forms of the ministers who officiated, together with the texts from which they preached, remained imprinted on his mind till his dying day. Another thing, too, he noted, and ever afterwards retained as his one reminiscence of the subject-matter of the sermons,—that the names of Charles I., Charles II., and James II., again and again recurred in the discourses of both preachers in emphatic and by no means complimentary terms. Such are the little shreds and patches of early reminiscence which, like specks of snow in the crevices of the hills, cling to the memory in all their vivid freshness from infancy to age, and which all the heat and glare of life's toilsome summer can never melt away. The kind of reminiscences which thus earliest, and with the greatest tenacity attach themselves to the youthful mind, were an interesting and not unprofitable subject of inquiry; and perhaps it is not the least argument in favour of such solemn commemorations of great national events as that above referred to, that however slight the impression they may often make on the adult mind, they do certainly, in a very peculiar manner, arrest the attention of the young, and prompt the eager inquiry, "What mean ye by this service?"

From the date of this incident the subject of this sketch began to take a more definite interest in the services of the sanctuary, and to carry away his recollections, less or more, of texts and sermons. The following notes in regard to the style of preaching practised in those days, taken from his memoranda, may be read with interest, as affording a glimpse into the interior of Scottish Church life seventy years ago:—"In those days," he writes, "it was not unusual to preach from the same text for successive weeks and months—a whole system of doctrine and of practice being opened up and reiterated from Sabbath to Sabbath. For example, the text being 'Repent, and believe the gospel,' several sermons were occupied in telling what the gospel was—its doctrines and its duties; then on 'believe,'—the evidences of the gospel, its truth and certainty; and next repentance was treated of, and its connection with faith, all under the same text." One does not wonder that under a system like this, "the giving out of a new text was quite an era; every eye and ear were stretched out and fixed; every Bible ready to be opened, as if it had been a 'latter will.' The new text comes, it is Jude 20, 21, 'Building up yourselves on your most holy faith,' &c.; again the truth to be believed was treated of, the nature of faith in connection with these truths, its holy character and influence, with the practical lessons thence resulting, &c. &c., in a long series of discourses stretching on from week to week. On this plan, no doubt, much sound doctrine was brought out, and the hearers, if not too impatient, got very good matter on which to meditate, but certainly the mode was not attractive, and superinduced tedium, while it did not do justice to the fulness and variety of the divine Word. Let it be observed, however, that the expositions of large portions of the Bible, by way of lecture, formed always the first part of the forenoon's worship, although the *reading* of a whole chapter was not at that time practised in any of the Presbyterian Churches as a regular part of the service. A younger minister, however, who at this time acted as assistant to the aged minister of the parish, introduced among us the new and certainly better method of giving a new text at least every second Sabbath. He went upon the maxim, '*bonus textuarius est bonus theologus,*'[1] and, accordingly, the first quarter or more of the hour or of the hour and a half consisted of parallel texts made to bear on the illustration of the passage in hand, after which he lightened, and even thundered. I have heard that this copious divine, on his removal to a church in England, found that it behoved him to abbreviate much to suit the English taste. The first half hour at least he had to cut off, and became, in respect of length, an ordinary preacher."

I learn, from the recollections of a younger brother of the family, that the system thus described was still in full force during the first quarter of the present century in the same church of Borrowstownness. Preaching from the text, "Behold, I stand at the door and knock," the then

---

[1] [Latin: "A good Textuarist is a good Theologian."]

minister of the parish, the Rev. Dr. Rennie, discussed, *seriatim*, from Sabbath to Sabbath, in separate discourses, the "bars" of the door at which he knocked; then in a fresh series the "instruments by which he knocked," and then, finally, the "uses" and corollaries derivable from the whole disquisition. In this way, and with the lengthened recapitulation by which each successive discourse was introduced, often so protracted as to render a very small portion of new matter needful, it will not be surprising that, as happened in the present instance, the Sabbaths of a whole quarter of the year were often consumed in the discussion of one single theme!

I am not quite sure if this singular style of pulpit instruction, so exhaustive, or rather exhausting, in more senses than one, be even yet in all quarters wholly and finally extinct. At least it was not so in my early school-boy days. I remember well that in a certain school, when on Monday mornings the master used to ask from his pupils the text of the sermon they had heard the day before, the children attending one of the churches of the place, came week after week with the unchanging, and, certainly, in one view, most comprehensive text, "The disciples were called Christians first at Antioch." Under this head, the congregation were doubtless favoured with a complete and systematic treatise on Christianity, its evidences and history, its doctrines and duties, its profession and discipleship, its responsibilities, claims, hopes, and fears, everything, in short, which could in anyway be included under the general idea of being Christians, or being called Christians, whether in Antioch or elsewhere. The custom is one, certainly, which posterity has very wisely let die; yet, perhaps, there is a danger lest, in the livelier and more desultory homiletics of modern times, we should err on the other side, and too much neglect that systematic and detailed instruction in Christian truth and duty at which our fathers aimed, and which, however imperfect in the mode of its conveyance, yet by its substance so largely contributed to form the solid and robust religion of former days. By all means let there be the new text each Sabbath-day, and a new vein of sacred truth opened up by the close, searching, and faithful exegesis of it, but, at the same time, let the order of subjects be so arranged that the whole circle at least of necessary truth shall be traversed within a certain, and not too extended time. After all, as old Tiff says (by the way one of the best professors of pastoral theology I know), the great end of all preaching is to show to poor strayed and bewildered souls, "the way to Canaan."[1]

After all, however, we much fear that the peculiarly prosaic style of preaching now described was at the time referred to not so much the result of any remarkable, zeal for the inculcation of saving truth, as of the flat, spiritless, and mediocre character of the age. It was a

---

[1] See an exquisite passage to this purpose in Mrs. Stowe's "Dred," a book which, even had it been more faulty than it is, the character and sayings of old Tiff alone might have rendered immortal.

sad time for the Church, at once intellectually, morally, and spiritually. The long and dreary night of the eighteenth century, though now drawing near its close, still maintained its reign, and even seemed to deepen in black darkness and death-like chillness, as it approached the dawn. It was only a year or two after this that the cause of Christian missions was ignominiously spurned from the table of the General Assembly, indicating, perhaps, the very lowest point in the thermometer of Christian faith and life within the pale of the Church of Scotland since the Reformation. Over vast tracts of the country, a cold, semi-sceptical moderatism held undisturbed sway, while the evangelism which here and there nominally maintained its ground was seldom of that strong, fervent, and high-toned type with which happily we are now so familiar. Error spoke aloud with clear and unfaltering tongue on the high places of the land, while truth, scorned and down-trodden, uttered its voice with stammering and muffled accents, and offered but a feeble resistance to the strong, triumphant tide of latitudinarian indifference that was rolling on. There was a good deal of nominal orthodoxy—fully more, perhaps, than a few years afterwards—but little holy unction, fervour, power. There were, however, even then noble exceptions amongst the ministry of those days, some of whom the subject of this sketch had heard and remembered, and whose names he often mentioned with honour. There was, for instance, the truly learned and holy John Gillies, of the College Church, Glasgow, who, entering on his charge in 1742, fresh from the revival scenes at Cambuslang, continued for six and forty years a singularly fragrant and fruitful ministry, and was now, full of years and of usefulness, bidding farewell to the Church below; and there was the ardent, single-hearted Robert Balfour, minister for forty years of the Outer High Church, Glasgow, "with his rich flow of hortatory eloquence and scriptural illustration, hampered, indeed, and restrained sometimes in the presence of a learned and fastidious auditory, but in his own congregation, or in other places, where he was at home, pouring out his whole heart, and flowing on through two or even three continuous discourses most seraphically;" and then there was the good and devout Archibald Bonar of Cramond, the worthy sire of a worthy race of fervent evangelists and doctors, who, though long trammelled by his MS.[1] preparations, to an extent which, in after life, he regretted, possessed, as Dr. George Hill once remarked to the subject of this memoir, "the most remarkable popular gift in preaching of any man he had ever known," and who, by his very psalms and prayers, apart from the sermon, created quite a sensation in congregations used only to the dull, uninspired orthodoxy of those days; then there was the strong, bluff, hearty, iron-fisted Bryce Johnston of Holywell—well known in the ecclesiastical arena as the formidable and uncompromising foe of moderatism,

[1] [Manuscript.]

at once keen in wit and strong in sense, now convulsing the Assembly by his inimitable picture of Balaam's ass in the character of the pompous and stately Dr. Carlyle,[1] now brandishing in his brawny hand a ponderous tome in the face of his adversaries, while he demolished their sophistries, till Dr. Hill cried out, "Take care, doctor; you'll strike our heads,"—but known still better in private life, and in his own immediate sphere, as a devoted Christian, and faithful, and fervent preacher of the truth; and finally, there was the warm-hearted and

[1] See Hugh Miller's graphic picture of the man and the scene in "The Two Parties, &c." "He (Dr. Carlyle, who for reasons well known, got the soubriquet of Jupiter Tonans) had been all his life long a keen supporter of Toryism. In his exertions to support the policy of Pitt and Dundas, he had, to employ the language of one of his brethren, who spoke for both the doctor and himself, 'risked even the friendship of his flock, and his own usefulness as a pastor among them.' He had taken a deep interest in the bill proposed in 1793 for the augmentation of ministers' stipends; it had been set aside, to his signal mortification, by his friends the Tories; and the reverend doctor, in the ensuing Assembly, proved unable to conceal his disappointment and chagrin. He went the length even of charging the ministry, in a style fully more lachrymose than pathetic, with 'ingratitude to their best friends;' and the complaint was ludicrously paraphrased in reply, by the singularly able and accomplished Dr. Bryce Johnstone, in the words of Balaam's ass, 'Am I not thine ass, on which thou hast ridden ever since I was thine until this day?' Dr. Johnstone followed up the allusion in a vein of the happiest ridicule, amid the irrepressible laughter of the house. The hint was caught by the eccentric Kay, and in his caricature, *Faithful Service Rewarded*, the reader may see a neatly-etched head of Jupiter Tonans, attached to a long-bodied, crocodile-looking jack-ass, bestridden by the late Lord Melville."—*The Two Parties, &c.*, pp. 24, 25.

courageous James Burn of Forgan, sometimes called, from his powerful and melting voice, and the use he made of it, "The Bell of Fife," a kind of Whitefield in his way, both in the system he followed, and in a kind of natural eloquence cast very much in the same mould. These, and such as these, including the goodly band of able and faithful men, to be hereafter mentioned, who then worthily represented the evangelical party in the pulpits of the metropolis, together with the Calders and the Frazers of the far north, were burning and shining lights in their day, all the more that they were so few and far between. Doubtless the very presence of such men within the bosom of the National Church served to preserve many a faithful soul within her pale, who had else sought spiritual food elsewhere, and kept alive, even in the darkest times, the persuasion that a blessing was yet in her, and would burst forth into life on another day. The lamp, though dim and flickering, still burned in the sanctuary, nor had the shekinah yet departed from the Holy Place.

CHAPTER II

1791–1799

BOYHOOD AND COLLEGE LIFE

And Jabez called on the God of Israel, saying, Oh that thou wouldest bless me indeed, and enlarge my coast, and that thine hand might be with me, and that thou wouldest keep me from evil, that it may not grieve me! And God granted him that which he requested.

—1 Chron. iv. 10.

THE preliminary training of the primary and of the grammar school was in those days quickly sped. Where all that was required previously to entering the university was reading, writing, arithmetic, and a small smattering of Latin, the brief curriculum was speedily run, and the schoolboy was drafted away to the college almost before he had entered on his teens.

Thus our halls of learning became what unfortunately they still continue too much to be, rather academies of boys than of men. Accordingly, we find the subject of our sketch as early as the year 1791, and when only in his thirteenth year, already passed from school life, and enrolled as a full-fledged undergraduate of the University of Edinburgh, under no less distinguished a teacher than Dr. Andrew Dalziel, and alongside of such notable compeers as John Campbell (now Lord Chancellor), and Henry Brougham. He passed his under-graduate course with commendable diligence and success, and entered the Divinity Hall in the winter of 1795. Here he pursued his sacred studies under the then Professors of Systematic Theology and Church History, Drs. Andrew Hunter and Thomas Hardie, in the former of whom he enjoyed the benefit of an edifying example and sound doctrinal instruction; in the other, the stimulus and healthful tonic of a keen, original, and richly suggestive mind. Of both these teachers he ever afterwards spoke with grateful respect,—but with peculiar affection and sympathy of the former, as not only the man of study but the man of God. But there were influences and scenes outside the hall, to which he recurred in after years with still livelier satisfaction, and which contributed in a much higher degree to form the character of the future pastor and watcher for souls. The holy fire was kindled, not by the lessons of the schools, but by a live coal from the altar of God. Amid the hallowing and soul-quickening atmosphere of Sabbaths spent in Lady Glenorchy's or Lady Yester's Church; the one under the ministry of the lively and fervent Thomas Jones, the other of the saintly and tenderly plaintive David Black—the M'Cheyne of those days—or in kindly personal colloquy in the study or at the breakfast table of such benignant fathers in the faith as Walter Buchanan and Thomas Randal Davidson, the smoking flax in his young heart, as in many others besides, was fanned into a flame of holy decision and courage which burned on through life. The two last mentioned worthies he especially commemorates as pre-eminently the students' friends. Not only did they notice and encourage pious or hopeful youths when directly thrown in their way, but positively laid themselves out for this kind of work, seeking out those young recruits of the sacred army "very diligently," gently rallying them around them, and both by loving counsel and substantial aid cheering them on to the holy conflict before them. How much good of the most precious kind was thus by them wrought unseen,—to how many a young soldier of Christ who in after days warred a good warfare, they spoke at the critical moment the word in season, the day alone will declare. Of these the subject of this memoir was one; and it is not more to perpetuate the remembrance of a type of character which has always been too rare among our city clergy, than to fulfil a long standing debt of gratitude, that we present the following brief touches of affectionate remembrance which I find recorded in his papers after the lapse of more than sixty years. They make no pretensions to the character of finished biographical sketches; but even a few random footprints of the noble and true-hearted of former days are too precious to be permitted to pass away.

Of Dr. Buchanan he thus writes:—"I really write this *'con amore*;' as of all the kind friends of young men prosecuting their clerical studies, he and his truly excellent lady were beyond doubt the most uniform and unwearied. The Doctor was a native of Glasgow, where he has still most respectable relations, was ordained first as minister of Stirling, and translated in the year 1789 to the Canongate Church in Edinburgh, where he laboured for nearly half a century. His well-known hospitable dwelling was in Reid's Court, Canongate, the centre house as you enter the court, a rather humble looking dwelling as times go now, but then, with its garden behind, convenient and respectable. An aunt of my own, a clergyman's widow, for some years occupied the corner house to the left of the court, which may have led to an earlier introduction to the worthy Doctor than might otherwise have been. Yet I am not quite sure of this, inasmuch as he and his worthy lady made it their object to find out students to whom they might be of use in every sense of the word. So it was; Dr. and Mrs. Buchanan were succourers of many, and of myself also. Dr. Buchanan's manner was engaging, and made raw and modest youths at their ease in his company. They were also introduced from the study into the parlour for breakfast or tea, and were encouraged to speak of their friends, and companions, and studies. They were presented, too, with books of more or less value, but all of course combining the *utile* with the *dulce*.[1] It is amazing how much good may be done in this way, and at no great expense. Inquiry was made where the young men attended public worship, and of the sermons which they heard. By the way, observing that a brother of mine (afterwards minister of Brechin), was in the way of going out to sermons on the Sabbath evenings, he cautioned him, recommending in preference the recollection of, and meditating on what he had heard, and the trying to do some good in the family in which he boarded. His kindness was more to be noted by us, inasmuch as we were not his hearers, although his church was near us, the greater popularity of Dr. Jones, whom we chiefly heard, not at all cooling his regard to us. Contemporaries who shared in his fatherly attention, were, *inter alios*,[2] Henry Grey,[3] Andrew Thomson,[4] James Brewster,[5] Robert Lundie,[6] George Cupples,[7] followed afterwards by a long catalogue, of whom 'many remain unto this present, and some have fallen asleep.'

[1] [Latin: *utile*=useful, *dulce* = sweet.]
[2] [Latin: among other people.]
[3] Of St. Mary's, Edinburgh.
[4] Of St. George's, Edinburgh.
[5] Afterwards of Craig, Forfarshire.
[6] Of Kelso.
[7] Of Stirling.

"Dr. Buchanan, having private means of his own, and, moreover, having a taste for what we may denominate a kind of evangelical alliance, long before the era of that happy association, was much in the way of making excursions to England, and forming acquaintance with the Simeons, the Venns, and the Rowland Hills of former days. He had more of the English address and mode of utterance, without, however, the least affectation, than most of the fathers and brethren of that time. He was tried, for the most part, with colleagues of a different spirit from his own, except in a few later years of his life, when the late well-remembered Dr. Alexander Stewart, first of Moulin and Dingwall, was admitted to the first charge, who, however, was soon removed by death (anno 1821). Dr. Buchanan himself died in 1833, being then in the forty-fourth year of his ministry there. Mrs. Buchanan survived him for several years, to old age, and died full of faith and good works, combining, in as high a degree as I have ever known, the qualities of the lady and the Christian, and leaving a blank in Edinburgh society not easily to be supplied. The annals of St. Luke's Church may be referred to as one, and the latest scene of that 'elect lady's' evangelistic gifts of zeal and love."

Our companion sketch is that of one of a harder, robuster make, but withal of as kind and true a heart. He had a rough rind, but the kernel that lay beneath was sweet and sound. Whatever brilliant and more striking gifts God may bestow on his Church, the world can ill at any time spare the goodly succession of such strong, erect, serious, clear-minded, and warm-hearted men of God as Dr. Thomas Randal Davidson:—

"He was son to the somewhat eccentric, but able and venerated Mr. Randal of Stirling, of whose more than magisterial command over the populace of that ancient burgh, and of the awe and dread which surrounded him on Sabbaths and week days, we have often heard.

"He took, as is well known, the name of Davidson as heir to his Uncle by the mother's side. When one wished him joy on his succession, he said, 'Wish me more grace, man.' A young relative of my own said, when he heard of Mr. Randall's succession to such a fortune, 'he'll preach nae mair.' Little, poor fellow, did he know of the man, and less of the power of the gospel, and its victory over the world.

"He was ordained minister of Inchture, near Dundee, and next admitted to the charge of Outer High Church, Glasgow, and, finally, one of the ministers of the Tolbooth Church, Edinburgh. When I, as a student of philosophy, was first introduced to him in the year 1793, he was the Rev. Thomas Randal, and lived in a house on the south-west side of St. James' Square. He, too, like Dr. Buchanan, was distinguished for his friendly and fatherly care over young men preparing for the ministry. He was not so engaging in his manner as Dr. Buchanan, but not less practical in his attention to their real interests. Among the first questions he put to me was—'If I had read any biographies of good men?' to which I answered, that I had read the life of Matthew Henry. He said, 'Philip's is better. Any other?' I said, 'I have read Leechman's Life' (Professor of Divinity at Glasgow). This did not please him. He said, 'Who put *that* into your hands?' This was rather a back set to me, and I replied rather abashed, 'I should like to get a reading of Philip Henry's life.' He said, 'There is Fraser of Brae's Life.' He then cautioned me against reading or buying books, *e.g.*, at auctions, without being ascertained of their real value. In 1796-7, being then a student of theology, he asked me if I was a member of any prayer-meetings, or of a theological society. I no doubt would tell him that I was a member of a prayer-meeting in the house of the widowed mother of George Wright, my fellow student (afterwards the worthy Dr. G. Wright of Stirling); where I met with John Campbell, well known years afterwards as the African traveller to Latakoo, and the zealous promoter of every good and holy work. As to the other question, I told him (the Doctor) that I was a member of the Old Theological Society, which met on Saturday evenings in the Divinity Hall. He was surprised, and said I should rather have joined the 'Philo-Theological Society,' which had the character of being composed of the more pious students; but when I asked him if he would advise me to leave the old and join the other, he said, 'By no means; that would look cowardly. You must just do the best you can to bring them to better views, and defend the truth.'

He recommended to have an interleaved Bible, and to note down critical and useful remarks, from reading or hearing, and counselled the practice of diligent and select serious reading, the improvement of time, early rising, &c.

"Certain it is, as my friend Dr. Guthrie has remarked somewhere, that the worthy doctor did help some of the more rustic students to a 'guinea's worth' of the training of a respectable teacher of graceful motion,—a Mr. Gibb, if I mistake not, a member of the Rev. Dr. Hall's Church, Rose Street, 'to teach the lads,' as he expressed it, 'to enter a room properly.' This *inter alia*[1] shows that the doctor was a practical man, and that he was observant of the minuter as well as of the graver and weightier matters.

"He insisted much on the importance of the manner of delivery in the pulpit. He said to myself that he thought he could trust the *matter*, but was jealous about the *manner*; which he insisted was not studied as it ought, by some of the preachers otherwise good and sound. As to gifts of books to poor students he was very liberal. On the subject of the reading of sermons in the pulpit, he said, 'Beware of even using notes, for I,' said he, 'began with a note the breadth of my hand, and now I cover almost the whole two pages of the Bible.' I had at first a kind of terror of Mr. Randal, but at length came to like him much; and, with many ministers living, and not a few gone to a better world, owe a tribute to his memory.

[1] [Latin: among other things.]

"What a life of activity and usefulness was his! In a conversation I had with him, early in my own ministry, he mentioned his having met with Dr. Blair in the course of a Saturday's musing on Salisbury Crags, when going over mentally, and sometimes orally, his subject for the morrow,—who, in a friendly way, asked, 'how it was that he, who had been a minister for some years previously to his coming to Edinburgh, was making such exertions in the way of preparation for the pulpit, having only one sermon a week to revise and deliver?—as to visiting, catechising, &c., such labours were not to be expected in the city, or even the visiting of the sick, which was left to elders and pious laymen.' 'That was his view of the matter,' said Dr. Davidson, 'and yet he was one of the best of them (the moderate clergy). I told him I could not take that view of the subject and that I considered that more of labour than ever was required to fulfil the duties now incumbent.' How many volumes might be filled up with the notanda of families regularly visited; of poor sick, sought out, comforted, and soothed; and of friendless youths instructed by books and by advice, as well as helped by seasonable pecuniary aid! When no longer able to mount the stairs in the houses, for instance, facing the passengers over the Mound from the New Town, ascending to ten or twelve tiers or flats, he employed and paid a probationer as his deputy to visit the indwellers in ordinary, as well as the sick and the dying. The following anecdote belongs to the period just before age unfitted him for this labour:—Three, perhaps four, young men, engaged in business, friends of mine, instead of taking lodgings, bethought themselves of renting a flat in the midway up the 'land of houses' referred to, and constituted, with an elderly servant, quite an unique kind of family. To the wonder and profit of the young men, *who* should make his appearance among them one day, but the worthy Dr. Davidson, giving them a pastoral visit in the course of his parochial rounds, observing at the same time that this was a novelty in his experience, a species of domestic society which interested him, and giving them pastoral counsels which I know were most thankfully received. The annals of eternity will show how much that devoted minister did in his days, in ways thus quiet and unobtrusive, in the cause of his blessed Master, and for the good of souls.

"Dr. Davidson, as to his bodily form, was of ordinary height, and rather slender make. As already hinted, he was an early riser, and very temperate in all things. He died in 1827, being in the 81st year of his age, and the 57th of his ministry, and forming, singularly enough, one of five amongst the clergy of Edinburgh about that time who had completed the fiftieth year of their ministry."

Truly, few ever better earned the crown of those who, by "patient continuance in well-doing," and in the great Master's sight alone, "seek for glory, honour, and immortality."

Amongst the other ministers, besides his special favourite Dr. Jones,—whose uncommon liveliness, as the little man rocked to and fro in the pulpit, into which he popped in from behind, and bounded along in his own fresh, buoyant, and fervent strain, at once attracted him,—our young student commemorates, with special zest, a Sabbath spent in Old Greyfriars' Church, under the massive, vigorous, and gravely serious John Erskine. Curiously enough, he sat in old Walter Scott's pew, and could thus verify, from the very point of view from which it was taken, the celebrated novelist's vivid photograph. The "black wig without a grain of powder," "the narrow chest and stooping posture," "the hands, which, placed like props on either side of the pulpit, seemed necessary rather to support the person than to assist the gesticulation," "the tumbled band," and "the gesture which seemed rather spasmodic than voluntary,"—all this, together with the strong masculine sense, and wise, weighty, pregnant words of the venerable preacher, vividly impressed him, and was recognised and welcomed in after years on the canvas of the great painter, as the familiar features of a friend. More fortunate, however, than Colonel Mannering, he was successful in getting a hearing also of his more celebrated colleague, Principal Robertson, and was much prepossessed by the calm and pleasant manner in which he pronounced those stately periods, with the rhythm of which we are all familiar. "He wrote his sermon on one side of the paper, in separate leaves, pushing gently the page he had read to the left side of the pulpit Bible. His text was taken from Psa. xxii. 23, 'Glorify him, all ye seed of Israel.' I remember two things besides his neat mode of reading, namely, that he recommended the Shorter Catechism, which makes glorifying God and enjoying him for ever the chief end of man; and remarked that the Heathen Greeks and Romans seem to have had a kind of shadowy idea of the connection between the two, when they represented the entrance to the temple of honour as through that of virtue." By the way, I find express confirmation in these memoranda of that characteristic anecdote in which tradition has embodied, and as it were enshrined, the distinctive character and spirit of these two distinguished men. "The Rev. Principal," so he relates the story, "one fore-noon had advanced the position, that 'so great is the beauty of virtue, that if perfect virtue should appear in a human form, all would fall down and worship her;' and the sounder colleague in the afternoon said, in allusion to this, 'That perfect virtue did appear once, and only once in a human form,—and *was crucified!*'"

One other vivid reminiscence of Erskine he retained through life,—the celebrated "Rax me the Bible" scene, in the Assembly 1796, at which he was present, and which may be placed beside Knox's sermon at St. Andrews, or Andrew Melville's interview with James, among the great historical pictures of the Church of Scotland.

Our readers will remember the worthy Dr. David-son's misgivings on the subject of our young friend's connection with the "Old Theological." From the sequel it appears, that his suspicions on that score were not wholly groundless. Its atmosphere was evidently charged strongly with opposite electric elements, which frequently came into loud, if not deadly, collision. The discussions, often on vital questions of the faith, were animated, vehement, protracted:—

"Among the members of the Old Theological Society of that day (1796-7), the most notable was the famous John Leyden. He came like a wild goat from the Lammermuir Hills,—his speech and action the most original and eccentric, without, however, the least affectation of singularity, of which he was wholly unconscious. Lord Cockburn, who was a co-member with him in another more scientific society, along with Henry Brougham, Horner, &c., has given a true and graphic description of him in those days. He and Logan (of Chirnside after-wards) always took the heterodox side in our debates. The worthy Donald M'Donald, Dr. A. Hunter's servant, or doorkeeper of the Divinity Hall, a zealous Highlander, seemingly one of 'the men,' overhearing us from behind the door when Leyden and Logan put forth their heretical spoutings, gave sometimes a significant knock (once I recollect he said he would fire a pistol among us), and by his plaudit and encouragement, cheered on those who spoke in defence of the truth. Leyden was very amiable in his native simplicity and originality, and became much more correct in his views of divine truth in after days. His future course and poetical effusions are well known, and his early death in India, in the very opening scene of his bright and useful career, is most affecting."

It is indeed a pregnant proof of the still dominant and triumphant position of the latitudinarian and Laodicean spirit of the age of Robertson, that it continued to draw to itself so large a proportion of the very flower and promise of the rising race. It was still the strong and gaining cause, and like every other strong and gaining cause, rallied around it the whole crowd of the weak and the wavering; while the intellectual and literary lustre which a few celebrated names had thrown around it, imparted to it a peculiar fascination for the young and the aspiring. It thus numbered in its ranks the great body of the brighter and more genial spirits of the time, as well as many others who were neither bright nor genial, but had a keen ambition, at least, to be esteemed such. It was, in fact, the religion of the court party, of the literary coteries, and of fashionable society. It was the religion of Principal Robertson, of Lord Melville, and of all the world, save only a few pious women, and old-fashioned, however worthy, and well-meaning ministers of whom fame knew nothing. It was, in short, the strong and central stream of the world, and even of the religious world; and therefore, by the simple force of its current, drew to itself and carried along with it all the straws. It is not surprising that the great majority of young and unformed hearts, however originally well disposed, gave way beneath this influence. Nothing, indeed, could stand before it but the most serious views and the deepest convictions of the truth. To resist was to pass at once beneath the shadow of the cross; was to go forth to Christ without the camp bearing his reproach. Well did the subject of this memoir remember long afterward the keen "ordeal of scorn" which the modest profession of evangelical sentiments cost him in some of the new town circles where he visited, and how even the mere fact of attending "such places" as Lady Glenorchy's or the Tolbooth Church provoked the wondering and contemptuous smile. In academic circles the prevailing tendency took a more theoretic direction. What in general society was Laodicean indifference and ungodliness, was here heterodoxy. A certain freedom and laxity of faith was the fashionable mode. The profession of a strict orthodoxy was deemed the mark of a mean and narrow spirit, a certain boldness of heterodox speculation and free thinking, the proof of a large and enlightened mind. So easy a road to intellectual eminence was sure to be well trodden. It is always easier to mount a badge than to fight a battle, to join a set than achieve for oneself anything good or great in any field of thought or action. So, while a few strong spirits were boldly broaching and defending error, the feeble crowd aped it. A good story illustrative of this my father used often to tell as having come under his own knowledge. A young country minister, of large vanity and small mind, eager to tread this ready road to fame, was in the habit of dropping hints among his friends that his orthodoxy on certain deep speculative points was not altogether to be trusted, and dabbled a good deal in the buying, or, at least, looking at books which he never read. In this way he came under the notice of a shrewd Edinburgh bookseller, whose shop he frequented during the Assembly sittings, and who seems at once to have taken his measure. He invited him to take tea at his house, giving him to understand that he would find there a literary reunion suited to his taste and his studies. On going there he was at once introduced to a grave and reverend senior whom he had never before seen, but whom he at once concluded to be one of the chief lights of the theological world. Accordingly, he fastened himself to this man for the evening, and was soon embarked on the wide sea of theological discussion and speculation. He modestly hinted his heretical doubts and misgivings, and was gratified beyond measure by the kindly interest with which his companion mourned his youthful aberrations, and hoped that he might yet live to embrace other and sounder views. After an evening spent much to his own satisfaction, he rose to leave, and in quitting the room, asked his host in a whisper, "Who is that reverend gentleman with whom I have been speaking most of the evening?" "Oh, do you not know who that is? It is the head beadle of the Tolbooth Church!"

Yet strongly as the tide of evil was still running, it was rapidly approaching its highest point, and was soon to commence its ebb. The very height to which the course of defection had now come, as in the sad Assembly of 1796, tended to startle the public mind and originate a reaction. The heart of the religious common people, as well as of the humbler middle classes, was still sound, and rallied strongly round those faithful men who, in the darkest times, upheld the standard of the truth. While the Robertsons and Blairs were the idols of literary coteries and polite circles, the real leaders of the people, and the exponents of the deepest religious consciousness of the time, were men of another mould. Hence it is that we find the evangelical party even then much more largely represented in the metropolitan pulpit, than the prevailing bias of men in power would have led us to expect. They were, in fact, the only men the people would hear,—the only men in whom they had any confidence whatever,—and in this whim, as a mere matter of governmental policy, they must be gratified. Thus we find contemporaneously at Edinburgh the following goodly band:—John Erskine, Sir H. Moncreiff, Wm. Paul, D. Dickson, sen., Walter Buchanan, Andrew Hunter, T. R. Davidson, Thomas Jones, and David Black[1]—all men of sterling worth and piety, all of respectable, some

[1] I find the name of Dr. John Campbell of the Tolbooth Church also mentioned in the memoranda before me, with great respect and regard, as one of the ablest divines and best men of that time; but he did not come to Edinburgh until 1806.

of distinguished, powers. There was not, indeed, among them any one man of commanding eloquence or fame, no thrilling voice like that of Guthrie or Chalmers, on whom crowds of all ages and classes hung enchained. They were of a class fitted rather for defensive, than for powerfully aggressive action, forming a strong and solid breastwork against the further progress of defection, rather than a gallant charging column to meet and turn the tide of war. Yet, such as they were, and for the special sphere and task assigned to them, they quitted themselves like men, and did their work bravely and well. If they did not kindle a flame they nourished and cherished the smoking flax. If they did not storm the citadel of the enemy, they at least held their ground before it till stronger reinforcements arrived. They sowed the seeds of the future harvest. They prepared the way for that great revival, which about the year 1810 or 1812, set decisively in, and which thenceforward, under such leaders as Andrew Thomson, Henry Grey, and Robert Gordon, steadily advanced to victory.

So much for the state of matters within the Established Church. Outside its pale, we begin at this time to descry still clearer fore-tokenings of the coming better age. While the regular lines, as we have seen, maintain a cautious, defensive position, a gallant company of irregulars are mustering apart and preparing for bold and resolute aggressive action. Greville Ewing,[1] John

[1] Originally of the Established Church, but seceded about this

THE PASTOR OF KILSYTH

Campbell, Robert and James Haldane, with other congenial spirits, are already in the field, as the pioneers and forerunners of that great company of preachers to the poor and the neglected who have since followed in their footsteps. The distribution of tracts, the founding of Sabbath schools, and the familiar and fervent preaching of the gospel in neglected villages, were their earliest enterprises, and owe to them, in Scotland at least, their first origination and impulse. The following brief but graphic notices from the memoranda before me will be read with interest, as one hails the first breath and earliest flowers of spring:—"In the year 1797 Mr. Greville Ewing and his dear friend Mr. Gairie of Perth (the worthy man whose presentation to the first charge of Brechin was set aside by the General Assembly, as not having studied regularly in any of the divinity halls of Scotland), a very holy man and useful preacher, set out on an itinerary tour for preaching and giving tracts. I learned from himself the following little anecdote. They had hired a gig and set out from Edinburgh on a fine summer morning having a large store of religious tracts to give away or scatter on the road during their progress. They came to Livingstone to breakfast. When standing on the landing step of the inn, Mr. Gairie looking

---

time, disheartened probably by the dominant spirit of error and indifference within the national pale. Others of less sanguine and impatient temperament, while equally mourning over the existing state of things, remained calmly at their post, and waited for better days.

about saw a venerable, hoary-headed man making way to them from the other side of the square, who said to them, 'Good-morrow, gentlemen; from Edinburgh, I presume?' 'Yes, sir.' 'Any news? we usually expect news from travellers from Edinburgh.' 'Oh,' said Mr. Gairie, 'old friend, here is the best news we have got,'—taking out a tract, 'Good News of the Way of Salvation,' written, I think, by Simeon of Cambridge,—'will you take one?' The old gentleman was, no doubt, taken by surprise— for the admirable essaying to do good in this way was just commenced—thanked Mr. Gairie, and went away with it. Mr. Ewing then asked his friend, 'Do you know to whom you have given the tract?' 'No, how could I know him? I never was here in my life before. Do you know him?' 'Yes, it is no other than the old minister of the parish.' His name was Wishart, one of the Wisharts of Kinneal old church, afterwards joined to Bo'ness. He was long a recluse, having gone through many domestic afflictions, and was by this time left alone. He used to say he was like a violin with all its strings broken. May we not hope the 'Good News' enlivened him in his solitude and in his declining days. He died in 1801.

"By the way, the same year, 1797, or the following, Messrs. James Haldane and John Aikman were itiner-ating and sowing the precious seed in the same way in Galloway. The following incident, which deeply impressed me at the time, I well remember. The gentleman in whose house I was residing as tutor came in one day from his ride, and told with great surprise that 'as he and pony left a watering trough, on the way, two gentlemen came up and succeeded him, when one of then handed him this.' It was the same tract, the 'Good News.' 'This,' said the major, is one of the strangest things I ever met with!' What blessings have followed the giving of such tracts the great day alone will declare fully."

The following anecdote of the late Legh Richmond belongs, of course, to a somewhat later year, but naturally connects itself with the above, as an interesting fragment of the early annals of tract distribution. I do not know if it has ever before appeared in print; if not, it well deserves recording as alike characteristic and instructive. It may be relied on as authentic. "On one occasion, as he with the other passengers in the public conveyance were ascending the well-known Moncrieff Hill near Perth, and left the coach to lighten the horses, and enjoy the magnificent prospect, he began to give a tract to any wayfarer he might meet. One of his fellow-travellers smiled when he saw one of the tracts given treated contemptuously by the receiver, torn in two, and thrown down on the road. 'See how your tract has been used,' said he; 'there is one, at least, quite lost.' 'I am not so sure of that,' said Mr. Richmond; 'at any rate, the husbandman sows not the less that some of the seed may be trodden down.' When they turned round at the top of the hill to take another look at the prospect before mounting the coach, they saw distinctly the fate of the little tract. A puff of wind had carried it over a hedge into a hay-field, where a number of haymakers were seen seated and listening to the said tract which one of their number had found. He was observed carefully joining together the two parts which had been torn asunder, but were held together by a *thread!* The devil had done his work imperfectly; for instead of tearing the tract to tatters, his agent had left it still available for use, a little pains sufficing to make it legible. Thus the poor man who had torn the tract in two was the means of its being read by a whole band of haymakers, instead of by a single individual. Thus, no doubt, moralized the excellent Legh Richmond."

"In the morning sow thy seed, and in the evening withhold not thy hand; for thou knowest not which shall prosper, whether this or that, or whether both shall be alike good."

It was indeed in a special sense *in the morning* that these brave hearts went forth bearing precious seed,— "very early in the morning, while it was yet dark." But the day-spring is near at hand; and those early risers are but the precursors of a great company who shall soon be awake and astir, and pressing with eager feet to the harvest field.

But returning to Edinburgh, and to the times and scenes between the years 1791 and 1799, it was amid influences such as we have described that our young student passed through his academic course, and gradually ripened from boyhood into manhood. He stood the ordeal well. Though of a calm and considerate, rather than determined temperament, yet he ever gravitated towards the right men and the right cause, and as by a gracious instinct assimilated whatever was good and true in the influences and associations round him. That he must have had his struggles more or less keen and protracted we cannot doubt, as indeed the allusion above to the "ordeal of scorn" sufficiently shows; but it is probable that that struggle was in his case less terrible and agonizing than in that of many others. At least in after life his religious course was a singularly calm and tranquil one,—rather a steady advance in good and resistance of evil, than a series of hard combats and death-struggles. As a student, too, he was, as ever afterwards, rather diligently and calmly conscientious, than in the highest degree strenuous—seldom doing his best, but always doing well. His bow was of good material and excellent make, but not often tightly strung, or drawn to its utmost stretch.

His theological course,—including a session at St. Andrew's under the distinguished Dr. George Hill, and another irregular one, in the course of which he spent some pleasant months at York, and formed an acquaintance with the excellent Mr. Richardson and the Church of England worship,—terminated in the spring of 1799, and he was licensed as a preacher of the gospel, by the Presbytery of Stranraer, a few weeks thereafter.

CHAPTER III

1800–1821

EARLY PASTORAL LIFE

'Tis now become a history little known,
That once we called the pastoral-house our own.
—COWPER

IN the bosom of a romantic dell, lying midway between the brisk seaport of Montrose and the fine old cathedral town of Brechin, in a narrow grassy plot left open between its two branching arms, stands, or rather stood, sixty years ago, the old church of Dun, with its little group of rustic mounds scattered at random around. On one side on a gentle rising ground on the further margin of the ravine is the manse, with its pleasant garden and glebe; on the other, reached by a high rustic bridge across the other and deeper water-course, the grey mansion-house, with its broad lawn and the grand old trees, and the bowling-green, where, tradition tells, the good Superintendent[1] and the stern John Knox used to disport themselves in hours of lightsome leisure three hundred years ago. It is the same church in which these worthies preached of old, and still contains a fine oak pulpit which tradition—though, I fear, mistakenly—connects with the same period. An intense stillness fills the place, increased rather by the incessant chorus of the rooks high over head, and the faint rush of the stream. It was in this gentle nook that the subject of these lines began his pastoral life on the 4th day of December 1800, with a parochial circle of some three miles diameter, and a population of 700 souls. The circumstances which led to this eligible settlement are curious. Early in 1799 it was rumoured in the neighbourhood that the old Laird of Dun, the then John Erskine, and the last of the name, was desirous to obtain a permanent assistant and successor for the aged incumbent of the parish, then laid aside from duty. My father's elder brother had been shortly before ordained one of the ministers of Brechin, and nothing was more natural than to think of the neighbouring parish as a suitable and desirable opening for his younger brother, then on the eve of taking licence. The question was, how to approach and obtain interest with the laird, in whose gift the living was? On consulting a friend, who

---

[1] John Erskine, Laird of Dun, and Superintendent of Angus under the early arrangements of the Reformed Church of Scotland.

knew Mr. Erskine's character and peculiarities well, "Just address him," said he, "direct, and write the *very best letter you can*; for the laird cannot write a letter himself,[1] and has, for that very reason, an extraordinary respect for any one who can." The advice was followed. Mr. Burns exerted all his epistolary talents in one grand effort, and dispatched his missive with the feeling, and, I do believe, with the simple faith also, of one who cast his bread upon the waters. It *was* found, but not after many days; for, at early dawn next morning, the clatter of hoofs was heard in the old Bishop's close, and presently the laird appeared at the manse door, demanding an interview with the minister. "You have sent me an excellent letter, Mr. Burns,—a most excellent letter; and you had better just send down the young man, and give us a trial of him, making no promises in the meantime." The young man did come, and discharged for the next twelve months all the duties of the parish open to him, to the satisfaction alike of the minister, the patron, and the congregation. Meantime nothing had transpired as to the succession; and matters remained in *statu quo*[2] till an incident occurred which at once decided the course of events. In the course of the year, there occurred one of those solemn days of public fast or thanksgiving in connection with the war which were then of such frequent appointment,

---

[1] It may be as well to say, in justice to the worthy laird, that this statement must not be taken quite literally.

[2] [Latin: the way it was.]

and there was service, of course, in the parish church. The laird happened to have some friends from a distance with him, by whose opinion he set some store; and he said to the party at breakfast, "We'll go over, and hear what this young man has to say on the war, and see what kind o' politics he has." It so happened that the young minister, somewhat over-tasked by this additional call on his resources, was thinking far less of politics and the war than the immediate urgencies of preparation. In his extremity, an old homily, delivered in the Divinity Hall, on the special providence of God, met his eye, and at once struck him as a suitable basis of profitable and seasonable instruction. He added a couple of sentences of befitting allusion to the circumstances of the day, and proceeded with it to the pulpit. The laird and his guests were delighted, not by the politics, but by the want of them; and concluded that the preacher was a discreet and modest, as well as a zealous youth. "Ye gave us a most excellent preaching today, Mr. Burns," said he, as he shook hands at the church door. From that moment his resolution was taken. Next day he mounted his horse, and called at the door of every cottage and farm-house in the parish to collect the general mind (one of the most attractive specimens, by the way, of lay-patronage we have ever heard of), and finding all fair and favourable, issued the presentation accordingly. An incident, however, curiously prophetic occurred on the day of moderation. When the call was produced to be signed by the people, the laird, of a somewhat slow and inapprehensive nature, deeming that all was done when the sign-manual of presentation had passed his hand, started, and said impatiently, "What is this now? Have I not signed the presentation? Surely nothing more is necessary!" He was with difficulty made to understand that "a paper called a call" was a necessary part of the decent forms of procedure in all such cases, and, with a faint murmur of protest, waived his objections accordingly. It *was* in these days a necessary form, but, in truth, little more. It was the organic remains of an extinct principle; or rather, as the future proved, the dry root of a great national right yet again to spring up and grow. How little did they dream in those days that those two documents then lying side by side on the table—the potent presentation on the one side, and the little insignificant scroll, with its dozen rustic names, on the other—were the representatives of two great principles which the intenser earnestness of another generation was destined to warm into life, and which, by their collision, should rend the whole fabric of the Scottish Church asunder, and give birth to the greatest religious revolution of modern times.

The simple annals of a country pastor's daily life are uniform and uneventful, and afford little scope for the biographer's pencil. Interesting and precious as any work done on earth in Heaven's eyes, it is the obscurest possible in the world's regard. Angels look down upon it; busy, eager, bustling men heed it not. A calm routine of lowly, though sacred duties, a constant unvaried ministry of love, it flows on in a still and quiet stream, arresting no attention by its noise, and known alone to the lowly homes it visits on its way, and the flowers and the fields it waters. The young pastor of Dun was no exception to this. He preached the word; dispensed the sacred supper; warned the careless; comforted the sorrowing; baptized little children; blessed the union of young and loving hearts; visited the sick, the dying; buried the dead; pressed the hand, and whispered words of peace into the ear of mourners; carried to the poor widow and friendless orphan the charity of the Church and his own; slipt in softly into some happy home and gently broke the sad news of the sudden disaster far away; lifted up the fallen one from the ground, and pointed to Him who receiveth the publicans and the sinners,—these things and such as these, he did in that little home-walk for twenty successive years day by day; but that was all. There is much here for the records of the sky, but nothing, or next to nothing, for the noisy annals of time. Such as the work was, however, he did it, as all who knew him witnessed, faithfully and well, with a calm, serious, conscientious, cheerful, loving diligence that was the fruit of faith and prayer; always at his work, and always happy in it, and desiring nothing better or higher on earth. He was happy in his neighbours. On the one side at Craig, at the distance of five miles, was settled, a year or two after himself, one of the dearest and most faithful friends of his life—the gentle, genial, and truly learned and godly James Brewster, brother of the more celebrated Sir David,—with whom, both in the ordinary interchanges of ministerial and social intercourse, and in random meetings in the library of Montrose, he spent many happy hours which remained green spots in the memory to the last.[1] On the other, separated from him only by a

---

[1] The history of his appointment to the parish of Craig is so curious, that I am tempted to transcribe the account of it from the memorials before me:—"The way in which it was brought about is a good story and true. The late Mrs. Ross, of Rossie, a lady of remarkable powers of mind, and attractive qualities of manner and mien, had erected at her own expense the handsome new church. She was aware of a serious barrier in the way of the settlement of the desired young man, but laid a plan for the accomplishment of the object. Having invited the then Lord Melville to Rossie Castle, she took his lordship to see the beautiful church, which his lordship of course highly commended. Mrs. Ross desired his lordship to ascend the pulpit to get a complete view. She then shut the door upon him, and presented her earnest petition to him, that as he admired the church, and at the same time allowed that a minister to occupy worthily and acceptably the pulpit was of prime importance (to which, of course, he assented), he would use his influence to procure from the college of St. Andrews, of which his lordship was Rector, a presentation in favour of Mr. Brewster. His lordship, in as smooth and courtly terms as possible, assured the lady, that were it practicable he would be most happy to comply with her request, but that the thing was absolutely impossible; that the professors had each in turn the appointment to the vacant livings in their gift, and that to any application from himself or any other person they would prove inexorable. But the lady was not thus to be put by. She kept his lordship a prisoner in the pulpit until he gave her his hand that he would do everything possible to gratify her wishes. He procured the gift of

---

narrow, moorish, border-land, was Logiepert, the home
and pastoral sphere of James Foote, afterwards translated
to the East Church of Aberdeen; a young minister then

---

two patronages to the college in lieu of this one, and so my friend
was ordained in due time." How long and faithfully he laboured
in the field to which he was in so singular a manner introduced,
the writer goes on to record with the fond ardour of a friend. For
one brief extract we must find room, from its interesting bearing
on the events of the present hour: "His addresses to the people of
Ferryden (a fishing village which his worthy predecessor, Dr. Paton,
told me had resisted all the attempts at reformation by himself and
predecessor), by tracts, and preaching among them, were attended
with a special blessing. This case affords one of the finest illustra-
tions of what Dr. Chalmers called the 'aggressive method,' and of
the powerful persuasive influence of domiciliary visits—in short,
through getting among them. Vain were all the efforts to induce these
fishermen to leave their village, and to come up from their own
Ferryden to the beautiful parish church, at only a mile's distance.
The fishers are a peculiar set of people. A visit from the minister at
distant intervals seemed like a kind of apparition, and to betoken
some sudden change among them; but when my friend set up a
chapel in the midst of them, and came down in the evenings, they
were greatly pleased—perhaps we should say flattered—and then it
was that something was gained. … It is worthy of notice that it is in
this village of Ferryden, at one time so very unpromising a portion of
the parish of Craig, that the Free Church (with which Dr. Brewster
cast in his lot) has the firmest hold—a rich reward for all the labour
he had bestowed on its moral and spiritual culture." It may now be
added, as a still more interesting circumstance, that this same spot
should have been one of the first and most highly favoured scenes of
the reviving showers that are now refreshing the land. Doubtless the
prayers of that man of God are being even now answered, and the
precious seed springing up which had been sown by his hand long
years ago. "Cast thy bread upon the waters, and thou shalt find it
after many days."

of great promise, and eminent acceptance, distinguished already by all those qualities of sterling worth, excellent gifts, and genuine warmth of heart, which won for him through life the respect and the love of all who knew him. To two other valued friends of those early days, living at a greater distance, but frequent visitants at Dun, he used often to recur in after years—William Hamilton of St. Andrews Chapel, Dundee, afterwards of Strathblane;[1] and Walter Tait, then of Tealing, and subsequently of Trinity College Church, Edinburgh. Both were frequent and ever welcome assistants at communion seasons; and by their fervent spirit and earnest words, far above the average tone even of the evangelicals of that day, created quite a sensation in the little rustic flock. The image of Mr. Hamilton's tall, impressive form, pacing up and down the manse parlour, and declaiming aloud the Olney Hymns, which were then first finding their way into Scotland, was long a cherished tradition in our family. Mr. Tait was then, and for many years after, one of the most devoted and extensively blessed ministers of that neighbourhood; both watering his own appointed vineyard well, and by his earnest voice attracting crowds of thirsty souls from all the parishes round. He made large reprisals on those brethren to whom his assistance was given—not only exacting the full regular payment at the stated times, but laying hold of them in behalf of his

---

[1] William Hamilton, D.D., father of Dr. James Hamilton, of the National Scotch Church, Regent Square, London.

people whenever a happy chance threw them in his way. Scarcely had a weary brother, halting by the way, got warm by the fireside, when the bell was heard swinging on the church belfry hard by. "What is that, Mr. Tait? surely it is not the bell ringing for church already?" "Oh, I suppose it is; the people, you know, will be expecting a word."

These, then, with his precious brother at Brechin, were the chief *dramatis personae* of a life-scene in which there was as much pure and unalloyed happiness, and as little of bitter sorrow, as is often allotted to man on earth. But another circumstance soon transpired which was more to him and to the future course of his life than all merely external environments. On the first day of the sixth year of his ministry, his home was brightened, and his life enriched by his union with one[1] who was in every sense "a help meet for him;" of whom delicacy forbids us to say more, and truth less, than that she was henceforth, for fifty-four unbroken years, his joy and strength, and that she "did good to him and not evil all the days" of their united life. Of a quick, buoyant, nimble frame, alike of body and mind, she was the direct counterpart of his staid and unimpulsive temperament; so that the one seemed expressly made to supply the lack of the other, and their loving companionship seemed the very alliance of motion and of rest, of calm peace and lightsome

[1] Elizabeth Chalmers, daughter of James Chalmers, Esq., proprietor of the *Aberdeen Journal*, Aberdeen.

gladness. Their first common sorrow was the death in infancy of their first-born son, whom they buried after a lingering and painful illness on the 3d August 1808,—an event of which I find the faint foot-print in the following entry: "Our dear child closed his eyes in peace on the 31st day of July, being Lord's day, in the afternoon while I was in church. My text that day was in Eccles. vii. 4, 'It is better to go to the house of mourning,' &c. My wife more composed than I could have expected. We trust that on this day our beloved son, and our first-born, entered into that rest which remaineth for the people of God; into that kingdom which is composed of little ones. We entertain the cheering hope that, through the merit of the blessed Redeemer, and according to the tenor of the covenant of grace, our child, whom we devoted to God in Christ, has obtained salvation, and now is added to the blessed company of the redeemed, singing the new song. He is moving in a higher sphere than he could have occupied on earth, and is receiving a much better education than we could have procured for him. He has made an early escape from the storms and tempests, the sins and temptations and sorrows of this mortal state. It is well with the child. Oh, may it be well with us!—may this trial (which we must long feel, many little circumstances recalling the remembrance of past joys) be made to work for good! The same afflictions are *literally* accomplished in my brethren, each of my married brothers having lost a son; two of them, James and Walter, an only son and a first-born. The mortal remains of our beloved John were laid in the dust on the afternoon of Wednesday the 3d of August 1808—immediately behind the pulpit, and above the remains of my aged predecessor, the Rev. James Lauder, who on the 14th of April 1802 had been laid in the grave, supposed to have arrived at the venerable age of 95. Thus the two extremes met—the early bud and the shock of corn fully ripe. Thus we have got 'a possession of a burying-place;' our first-born has taken possession of it in our names. Oh, may we be prepared to follow! may our lives henceforth be more useful, more spiritual! (Thus wrote the celebrated Dr. Doddridge in his sermon on the death of an amiable child aged about five, and thus I would also write.) On the Sabbath following I preached on Heb. xiii. 8, 'Jesus Christ the same yesterday, today, and for ever;' contrasting the unchangeableness of the Redeemer with the fleeting nature of all earthly things. *Omnia mutantur, nos et mutamur in illis;*[1] but Jesus Christ *semper idem, in secula seculorum*[2]—

> 'I am the first, and I the last,
>   Through endless years the same;
> I AM is my memorial still,
>   And my eternal name.'

Here is firm footing, this is the solid rock, on which we would build, which resists all the beating of the winds and waves of time and change."

[1] [Latin: all things change, and we change with them.]
[2] [Latin: always the same, forever and ever.]

This, however, was the only break for twenty years thereafter in that happy home. It was necessary, doubtless, in his case, as in that of others, to impart to the soul that deeper and tenderer tone which the untouched heart never knows. With this single interruption, the course of his life, domestic and pastoral, flowed on tranquilly; the quiet routine of daily work being broken and diversified only by such incidents as are familiar to every Scottish clergyman's experience. A ride to the neighbouring market town, and friendly chat with a brother minister in reading-room or public library; the stated resort to Presbytery or Provincial Synod; an occasional journey to a distant communion; a missionary meeting at Montrose; a missionary sermon at Dundee; the annual or biennial pilgrimage to the General Assembly, in days when the man sent was generally the man that would go, taking a line of friendly manses on the way—Tealing, Dairsie, Markinch; a rare windfall from the great world in the shape of a travelling missionary,[1] or literary explorer,[2]

[1] He records with special zest a visit of this kind by John Campbell, the African traveller, with another congenial friend.

[2] The elder M'Crie was in this way once his welcome guest, while engaged in collecting materials for the Life of Knox. The circumstances were somewhat curious. My father, at the doctor's request, had made application to Mr. Erskine for permission to explore the papers in the repositories of the Dun family, bearing on the Reformation period. The laird consulted his provincial man of business, who gave this worldly-wise advice: "Let no man in among your papers, Mr. Erskine, least of all the parsons. You can't tell what discoveries they may make about the estate or the teinds of the

pitching with him for the night; and last, but not least of all, the arrival of the monthly magazine weeks after the time, with all the keen speculation as to the author- ship of articles and letters, and the deciphering of initial marks and hieroglyphic signs;—such were the occasional *events* of wider interest which in those quiet days, far more than now, added zest to home duties and home joys, and, like gentle eddies from the great sea, freshened the peaceful creeks and bays of life.

A few jottings, culled almost at random, from a brief journal begun soon after his ordination, will give a more distinct idea of the daily ongoings of that quiet, but busy and useful life, we have endeavoured to sketch. Amid closet duties, studious hours, parish work, home joys and cares, readings in Erasmus, Burnet, Cotton Mather, and John Newton, with the Christian Instructor[1] and the Edinburgh Review, the days and weeks, even in that retired nook of the world, flowed swiftly on:—

"*Sept.* 15, 1808.—Visited Margaret Burley, a poor old woman in the Muir, whom I have frequently seen. She is nearly blind; a great aggravation of her other

---

parish. But there's that box containing the papers of the ___ estate (a property recently come into the family), let them take their will of them." So it was settled, and Dr. M'Crie only spent a pleasant leisure day at the manse, looking across wistfully now and then to the mansion-house with its papers, as a hungry dog eyes an inviting bone beyond the reach of his chain.

[1] Of this excellent periodical, as well as of its predecessor, The Religious Monitor, he was a regular reader, as well as a frequent contributor to their pages.

trials—widowhood, poverty, &c. Spoke to her of the importance of having the mind illuminated, the heavenly eye-salve, &c.; seemed attentive; prayed, &c. This day read for the first time Dr. Beattie's beautiful poem, the Minstrel,—a high entertainment; many just observations on life, beautiful moral painting, lively and striking description of nature, &c. Read portion of Erasmus' Enchiridion; Treatise on Spiritual Armour; many good thoughts, but rather fanciful and allegorical. In the evening reading aloud, &c.

"*Sept.* 16.—Rose at six. Read three beautiful hymns of Cowper's, Ps. lxxvi., Col. ii.; joined in prayer with E—. In good health and spirits. Read part of Deut. xiv. in Hebrew; family prayer; breakfast; worked in garden; read portion of Greek Testament; Erasmus; wrote notes on Deut. xiv. as a preparation for Sabbath work. Much reason to be satisfied with this plan of reading a chapter and making a few remarks on it, which does not supersede the ordinary lecture or exposition. In the afternoon I began, a few weeks ago, to read through the Psalms, and to comment on them briefly, besides the sermon. The advantage is, having more of the sacred oracles brought into view, which are the grand sources of divine knowledge and spiritual improvement. There is a deplorable ignorance of the Scriptures prevalent among us. I hope also, in this way, by the divine blessing, to set forth the beauties of the Scriptures, that they may be more diligently studied by my people at home; and to show how admirably fitted they are to convey instruction in all the various circumstances of life and of society. At Brechin, Forfar, and other places, this ancient and useful practice has been of late revived, and 'tis devoutly to be wished it were universal. With this part of my Sunday labours I have always reason to be satisfied; for what can be surer ground than the foundation of the apostles and prophets?

"Dined half-past three. I purchased this day Mather's Essays to do Good, revised by Burder; a golden little treatise, which I read some time ago with great pleasure, mixed with shame and regret that I had done so little good, which might have been at least attempted. Resolved, through divine strength, to review it carefully, to keep it by me, and follow, as far as practicable, the means of doing good which it prescribes,—the noblest of all studies certainly!

"In afternoon read aloud a chapter of Mrs. Rowe's Devout Exercises, Fuller's History of the Church in Britain,—a curious and entertaining work. Read chapter about abbeys founding, &c.

"*Sept.* 17, 1808. Saturday.—Rose a little before six, after a good night's rest. Thoughts wandering while dressing;—too usual with me. Read two Olney Hymns, and part of Ps. lxxviii., with Col. iii. and iv. Prayer. Ah, how cold and listless! Would that I could say with the psalmist, 'My heart is fixed, my heart is fixed.' Delightful morning, though heavy dews. This day important as preparatory for the solemn work of tomorrow. May my thoughts be well regulated, my affections devout, memory retentive. This day should preach to myself, that tomorrow I may be prepared to preach to others. This kind of preaching most difficult, but most important to the success of the other, &c.

"*Sept.* 18. Sabbath.—Rose a little after six. Read and expounded Deut. xiv. with some pleasure; preached from Luke xxiv. 34, 'The Lord is risen indeed.' Showed the doctrines and duties which follow from the resurrection of Christ;—his divinity proved; truth of the doctrine, and proved efficacy of the atonement; enemies conquered; resurrection of his people; heavenly-mindedness; right improvement of the Sabbath, the day on which he rose; preparation for his second coming. Afternoon and evening at Brechin (my brother preaching here) from Phil. i. 21, 'To me to live is Christ.' Some pleasure in the work, especially in the evening; large audience; subject very important; showed the nature of spiritual life; the author and object of it; Christ at once the object and the spring of all Christian activity and enjoyment. Inferences: 1. Who are Christians? 2. Excellency of Christianity. 3. True use and improvement of life, &c. Rode home, and got safely to my resting-place by eight, finding all well."

"Evening comes on. *Eheu fugaces!* Ah, how quick the lapse of time! Day after day steals on. Lord, teach me to number my days, that I may apply my heart to wisdom. The sun setting beautifully, yet how soon the glory fades away! Time now for meditation."

"Saw Miss A——.; in a poor state of health, but in a very comfortable state of mind. Pleasant—but ah, how rare!—to see the soul prospering while the body is weak and languishing,—cheered and enlivened by the precious promises, and joyful in hope of glory. Prayed with her, and with more pleasure and comfort than usual. Visiting sick is a most useful, and, in some instances, most agreeable part of duty. There much is to be learned. Newton, in his admirable letters, compares the utility of this exercise to a minister, to the infirmary and hospital to the surgeon."

"Newspapers. Rather more unfavourable accounts from Portugal than we expected. Our victory there turns out to be next thing to a defeat. Where these things shall end who can say? The Lord reigneth. As Portugal and Spain have so much blood on their heads—Inquisition, and ravages in the New World—there is reason to fear about them; but, at the same time, who can wish success to their rapacious and unjust foes? Who can but pity the poor, oppressed, and plundered inhabitants? What ground of thankfulness that we enjoy our privileges undiminished! Read Fordyce on Art of Preaching; very sensible and spirited: Fuller on Suppressing of Abbeys. Wrote to Mr. Brewster on birth of his third son. Must study more methodically, and visit more among the people. This day rather irregularly spent as to study. Notes for sermon. Read some admirable things in Essays to do Good."…

"Saw a poor diseased boy in Common Muir; exhorted and prayed; seemed peaceable and submissive. An affecting sight, to see the decrepitude of age in a youthful form, and death making advances in so humbling and ghastly a shape! Poor boy! may the Physician of great value heal the disease of thy soul, and then, no matter what comes of the frail and corruptible tabernacle. The sooner you get quit of it the more pleasant. What a glorious change must take place at the resurrection on such a vile and decrepit earthly body! He had been reading a sermon of R. Erskine's on the resurrection, 'All that are in their graves,' &c. Company at dinner; pretty agreeable; and if not so much useful conversation as might be wished, yet not offensive, or impure, or censorious. This is so far good. Mr. and Mrs. P—. stayed all night. Some useful and entertaining cracks. Oh! to be more edifying to one another when we meet! Much need to pray, 'Lord, guide our conversation aright!'"

"Read paper, and part of sermon on 'Whom have I in heaven but thee?' May this be my choice and portion! Oh, to have the affections regulated! How wandering the thoughts, and cold the desires! Lord, increase my faith! warm my cold heart! turn away mine eyes from beholding vanity!

"My wife employed in making clothes for the poor out of small pieces of cloth, &c. Much comfort in contributing to their warmth. 'It is more blessed to give,' &c. Did we only see how poor people are situated, it would stir up to do something, to study plans for their relief. To do good let us not forget; nay, let us seek occasion. Much to be regretted that doing good is not more reduced to a system, so as to be always in view. Lord, prepare me for thy work and service tomorrow, that I may not be dry and unedifying to others, and dull and comfortless in my own soul!

"Read Olney Hymns, chapters, and Hebrew. Newspaper. Prepared a subscription paper for poor woman. Called at House of Dun, with a view of getting something: not at home. Saw A— T— about getting poor woman, M— B—, provided in a small house. Called for A— N—, old woman, Muir, and conversed a little with her. A— T— in Muir. Found him a little better; conversed with him in the field. Found he had liked Walker's Sermons which I had lent him. Hope they may be useful." …

"Read Hebrew; Doddridge's Letters; composed part of sermon on 2 Cor. viii. 9, 'Ye know the grace,' &c.;—a noble subject! Oh, to speak as one that knows the grace here mentioned, that others may be affected with it! May we obtain such views of the glory and the grace of the Lord Jesus Christ, as may warm our affections and increase our love to the Redeemer and to one another. … Conversed with several people with a view to communion. Most of them want expression and clearness, which I'm afraid is owing to a defect in the affections. Too much outward in their views of religion; little heart work. Where all are so much alike, it is not easy to except any particular individual. Spoke to them for the most part individually, and endeavoured to be faithful; but it is amazing how coolly most of them receive these advices." …

"Saw E— C— at Mill; confined upwards of a year to bed; views still, I fear, but dark; seems to have no doubts of her salvation, or the least fear of death; but, alas! in too many we find this, without any apparent fitness or clear evidence of interest in the Saviour. I have often spoken very plainly to her, but I fear no radical change. Oh, for grace to be faithful! Read Cecil's Life of Newton,—very good; Doddridge's Letters; Burnet's History of his own Times, &c."

"Read Edinburgh Review on Clarkson on the Abolition of Slave Trade;—highly interesting. Mr. Clarkson deserves to have his name in the list of those great and good men who have laboured with indefatigable perseverance in the grand cause of humanity and religion, &c."

"Examined families at T—; four exhortations with prayer; not much satisfaction; sadly ignorant and insensible. Knowledge seems as low there as in any part of the parish. Being far from church, less known; much discouragement in the work, but *nil desperandum*,[1]— must labour and pray more. Lord, I beseech thee, send now prosperity!" …

"Read Edinburgh Review—article on Ireland; very

[1] [Latin: do not despair.]

instructive. Population of Ireland five millions and upwards; wonderful increase for the last forty years,— owing chiefly to living on potatoes, early marriages, &c. Prospect of affairs in Ireland very alarming. Their emancipation strenuously recommended in Edinburgh Review, as the only likely means of attaching them to us, and preventing them from becoming a province of France. Subject worthy of attention. To remove their ignorance and superstition desirable. Present system of keeping down by military will not do always. Certainly our most vulnerable point."

"Some pleasant moments of meditation and prayer with E—. Twilight the time allotted. Solemnizes the mind, and prepares for serious work."

"Preached on the words of Peter, 'To whom shall we go?' Have given up the use of notes in the pulpit; and though not perhaps so accurate, yet, upon the whole, more comfortable. Get more good from my sermons to my own mind; when trusting to notes, apt to pass away; mind not imbued with it; impression not so savoury or permanent. Upon the whole, I resolve to continue for some time without notes, though the memory often proves treacherous; hope it may improve; and when the mind is more stored and engaged with religious truths, will flow more easily. Oh, to be more spiritually minded, and to speak more from the heart, from experience, and with affection! A meeting (with the young) at three, for reading the Scriptures, examination, &c.; a useful work.

Pleasant thoughts in the evening, and conversation with E——. The Sabbath evening a delightful season when we are alone. Expounded in the family Ps. lxxi., and spoke to the servants. Examined the girl about the sermon; warned against sleeping and inattention. Stormy night. Poor sailors afar off on the sea!"

"Comfortable day, and I hope useful. Evening spent in meditation, conversing, &c. Explained Ps. lxii., and spoke to servants. Oh, may I love this blessed day, the best of all the seven!"

"Dined at Mr. M——'s; present, my brother and Mr. and Mrs. E——; some useful discourse, though might have been better. Too much about absent brethren; a fault among clergy."

"Read part of Gerard's Scripture Criticism. May be useful, though only out-works. A critical skill very desirable; but to imbibe the true spirit and influence of the truth, how much more to be sought! This writer seems to have no notion of any spiritual illumination, or higher teaching than man can give or acquire. But let my prayer be, 'Open thou mine eyes, that I may behold wondrous things out of thy law.' He recommends candour, &c., but no word of prayer or divine teaching. This, with some learned men, is accounted rank enthusiasm. May I experience much of that enthusiasm, and receive that knowledge of sacred truth which critics often want,— which John Newton seemed to have in no small degree,— the art of turning everything to spiritual nourishment and practice; a knowledge which purifies and warms the heart, and transforms into the divine likeness."

"Letter of Newton, after worship and prayer; subject, his visits to the sick, which he compares to the surgeon visiting the hospital: some very striking cases of the power of divine grace and divine teaching. Ah, how few such instances do we meet with! yet all with us profess to have hope at the last, and talk with great coolness about death and being with Christ. *I never met with one afraid to die*, though I have met not a few who, to all appearances, had reason."

"Saw E— C— at M—. Seems to have no fears of dying; yet I can scarcely discern marks of Christianity sufficiently clear and strong to warrant this. A cool acknowledgment of being a sinner like others, and a general trust in the merits of a Saviour, are all I can find. No lively faith, warm love, or genuine humility of heart. Prayed. Very difficult case to manage. Have spoken to her plainly my doubts about her; *she has none*. Oh, that she may be kept from self-deceit! Much wisdom, zeal, and courage needed in visiting the sick. Alas! how deficient am I in all these! Lord, increase my faith! inflame my cold heart! Enable me rightly to divide the word of truth, and to use great plainness of speech!"

"Pleasant, at the close of a day, to think of any good done, or at least attempted;[1] but as to the manner of doing, and the degree, what cause of humiliation!" …

[1] This idea, or rather this conviction and impulse of the heart, may be said to have been the key-note of his life from first to last.

And so, from day to day, amid loving thoughts, and kind deeds, and cheerful industry, and continual aspirations and strivings upward and onward, the quiet current of those happy, peaceful years slid away.

As to ministerial success in the highest sense, I find few decisive traces belonging to this period. The tone of religious life in the parish and the country round was not high. They were a decent, regular, church-going people—commendably observant of all the outward and routine duties of religious profession, but in few cases searching deeper or rising higher. There were few that "called upon God; that stirred up themselves to take hold of him." Family worship was rare, the decided profession of personal godliness rarer. As a general rule, and with very few exceptions, open ungodliness reigned in the hall, dead indifference in the cottage, and languor and listlessness in the church. Still there were blessed exceptions. Here and there, even then, there were consistent and shining disciples; here and there souls truly seeking God, and following hard after him. There were those among the crowd that were eagerly intent to touch the hem of Christ's garment,—hungry hearts that could not be content with husks, but must have the living bread. Such was one, for instance, who thus once gently chid her pastor when he had been dwelling, as she thought, too much on more general themes: "O dear sir, what aileth thee at the glorious surety righteousness of Christ?" To such hearts the pastor's words of deepest instruction and holiest wisdom came not in vain. Such were his joy and his encouragement then, even as they are now his crown in the presence of his Lord. It was at an after time, however, and in another field, that he was to reap a great harvest, such as now he had not learned to conceive of even in his dreams.

That whole history has drifted back into the far past. In visiting those early and well-remembered scenes a year or two before his death, he describes himself as one walking up and down in a land of the dead. A short time ago I too found my way to that quiet and solitary churchyard. The old church, superseded by a modern structure at some distance, had been turned into a tomb, but all around remained unchanged as in other days. But the congregation of the old pastor was beneath my feet. A solitary loiterer was standing near, who, to my inquiry, replied "that he remembered the name of a Mr. Burns; that one of that name, he believed, had once been minister there." Such is the scanty record on earth of so many years of faithful service, of so many prayers and unwearied ministrations of love!

But the young pastor was meanwhile gathering strength and experience for a wider and worthier sphere of service; and that sphere was in due time opened to him, by his appointment to the large and populous parish of Kilsyth, to which he was admitted on the 19th of April 1821.

CHAPTER IV

1800–1821

THE NEW CENTURY AND THE NEW AGE:

A RETROSPECTIVE GLANCE AT THE TIMES

Ev'n now we hear with inward strife,
A motion toiling in the gloom—
The Spirit of the years to come,
Yearning to mix himself with life.
—TENNYSON

THE world and the church had both advanced a long stride on their way, while those twenty tranquil years of pastoral life at Dun were running their course. They began, indeed, at a deeply interesting and eventful epoch. It was not only the commencement of a new century, but the opening of a new era—one of those critical moments in the moral history of the world in which all old things seem to be passing away, and all things to become new, and which, as by a deep and broad line of separation, cut off the future from the past. A new spirit seemed to breathe over the face of European society, and to quicken all the pulses alike of intellectual, moral, political, and religious life. Startled by the sudden shock of great events, and at the same time, doubtless, stirred inwardly by influences of a deeper and more mysterious kind, the nations awoke from the slumber of generations, and men everywhere began, as from a dream, to rub their eyes and look around them. The frivolous shallowness, the death-like torpor of the last age, was passing away, and giving place, among men of every rank and class, to a more serious tone of thought and feeling, in regard to all matters of vital concernment; which, as time wore on, sank deeper and deeper into the heart of society, and gradually infused into the whole framework of the world that element of moral reality and earnestness which constitutes the grand distinction between the nineteenth century and the eighteenth. It was, in fact, the expiring of one age and the birth of another—like that mysterious change which takes place in each diurnal round, during that solemn interval between the night and the morning which all watchers in sick-chambers know so well. "Everybody," says a singularly striking and suggestive writer, everybody at least who has watched by a sick-bed, knows that days have their appointed times, and die as well as men. There is one awful minute in the twenty-four hours, when the day palpably expires; and then there is a reach of utter vacancy, of coldness and darkness; and then a new day is born, and earth, re-assured, throbs again. This is not a fancy; or if so, is it from fancy that so many people die in this awful hour ('between the night and the morning,' nurses call it); or that sick men grow paler, fainter, more insensible? I think not. To appearance they are plainly washed down by the ebbing night, and plainly stranded so near the verge of death that its waters wash over them. Now, in live minutes the sick man is floated off and is gone; or the new day comes, snatches him to its bosom, brings him back to us, and we know that he will live. … Ah! blessed Morning, I am not ungrateful. That long-legged daughter of mine, aged eight years at present, did you not bring her back to me in your mysterious way? At half-past two we said 'Gone,' and began to howl. Three minutes afterwards, a breath swept over her limbs; five minutes afterwards, there was a blush like a reflected light upon her face; seven minutes, and whose eyes but hers should open, bright and pure as two blue stars! We had studied those stars, and read at a glance that our little one had again entered the House of Life.

"Our baby's dying and her new birth are an exact type of the death and birth of the day. One description serves for both. As she sank away, fainting and cold, so night expires. This takes place at various times, according to the season, but generally about two o'clock in the morning in these latitudes. If you happen to be watching or working within doors, you may note the time, by a coldness and shuddering in your limbs, and by the sudden waning of the fire, in spite of your best efforts to keep it bright and cheerful. Then a wind—generally not a very gentle one—sweeps through the streets—once. It does not return, but hurries straight on, leaving all calm behind it. That is the breath that passed over the child. Now a blush suffuses the east, and then open the violet eyes of the day, bright and pure, as if there were no death in the world, nor sin."[1]

If there be aught fanciful in the idea conveyed in these exquisite lines—or rather in some of the circumstantial details in which it is embodied—as regards the death and the birth of natural days, it holds true, unquestionably, in regard to the death and the birth of those epochs and ages which are the true days of the world. There are moments when the whole frame of things in the sphere of man's higher life seems "decaying and waxing old, and ready to vanish away;" and then again it awakens and starts forward with a bound to a new stage of its destined race. In the present case, the critical moment, "the one awful minute" of pause and transition between death and life, lay probably somewhere between the ninetieth and the

[1] From a remarkable paper in the Second Number of the Cornhill Magazine, entitled, "An Essay without end."

last year of the century—nearer, perhaps, to the former than the latter. At the beginning of that decade the night was at its very depth of chillness and utter gloom; before it closed, the morning breath had swept over the world. During the same interval, too, there passed away most of those faithful witnesses who, during the latter half of the century, had maintained the standard of the truth in evil days; as if washed down by the refluent tide of the expiring age to which they belonged, and in which their generation-work was done. John Wesley died in 1791; Bishop Horne, in 1792; John Berridge,in 1793; William Romaine, in 1795; Henry Venn, in 1797; William Cowper, in 1800;—as if entering one by one on their rest either at early dawn or break of day. John Newton lingers a little while behind, as a connecting link between the old generation and the new; but in seven years more he, too, is summoned home.[1] Meanwhile another band of like brave spirits have been coming forward in their place, to fight the same battle, amid more stirring scenes and in a wider and more conspicuous sphere. The tide quickly turns. Evangelism, hitherto an obscure and scouted sect, skulking in by-ways and in corners, and confined almost exclusively to the lower floors of social life, climbs upwards, and vindicates for itself a place in the highest circles and most influential spheres in the land. It had found for itself at least one powerful voice to plead its cause in the British Parliament; and at one of the great

[1] Died 1807.

Universities its standard had been planted, amid general contempt and opposition, indeed, but manfully and decisively, by one who for full fifty years held it aloft before the *elite* of the British youth. By the opening of the century the morning had fairly dawned. In the State, Wilberforce is in the very zenith of his influence and his fame. In the Church, Charles Simeon has fought fairly through his first struggles at Cambridge, and has nobly maintained his ground. Scorned, calumniated, persecuted, shrunk from, as a man proscribed and infected, he still holds steadfastly on his way, in the face alike of frowning dignitaries, riotous gownsmen, and hostile parishioners. Master of one pulpit close to the gates of the University, he is fast advancing on the tide of a rising public sentiment to his rightful place in the great St. Mary's itself. Gradually, timid disciples come forth from their halls and colleges to range themselves on the side of the truth, and the aisles of Trinity Church fast fill with gownsmen. At the same time, and in the same place, another powerful voice—the most eloquent in England—was pleading the cause of evangelical truth and true liberty in those magnificent orations which, in their kind, remain unrivalled in the British pulpit to this day.[1] Meanwhile, in an humbler sphere, the brave Rowland Hill pursues rejoicingly his evangelistic work in Surrey Chapel; and the Haldanes, with their "good

---

[1] Robert Hall was at this time in the very zenith of his career at Cambridge, a few years before the first sad eclipse of his noble genius.

news," traverse the length and breadth of Scotland; while far away in the distant East, William Carey and Claudius Buchanan, the leaders of a noble band, are already in the thick of battle on the high places of the heathen field. In 1797, the Practical View of Christianity was published. In 1799 the Church Missionary Society was founded. Other kindred institutions had either preceded it by a few years, or speedily followed.[1] As time drew on, the morning grew and grew. In 1805 Henry Martyn sailed for India. In 1806 the Slave Trade Abolition Bill was passed. In 1811 the tongue of Thomas Chalmers was first unloosed to preach the truth. In 1817, the Astronomical Discourses were published, and ran a race of popular favour and rapid circulation with the Tales of my Landlord. Meanwhile, the friends of evangelical religion multiply everywhere; faithful ministers increase; books of serious piety, with or without the charm of genius, are published, and eagerly

[1] The following are the statistics:—

Methodist Missionary Society, instituted,	1786.
Baptist Missionary Society, instituted,	1792.
London Missionary Society, instituted,	1795.
Scottish Missionary Society, instituted,	1796.
Church Missionary Society, instituted,	1799.
General Assembly of Church of Scotland's Committee on Foreign Missions,	1825.

Previous to this period the only society for missionary objects in this country was "The Society for the Propagation of the Gospel in Foreign Parts," instituted 1701, in connection with the Church of England, and which still exists, dividing with the Church Missionary Society the support of the friends of missions within the Episcopal pale.

bought up and circulated; Legh Richmond's tracts, Bickersteth's treatises, the Olney Hymns, and Foster's Essays, have each their mission and their work, and travel hither and thither in thousands over the land; the tone of religious and moral feeling throughout society at large sensibly rises, and everything seems to presage the speedy advent of a day of spiritual life and refreshing, such as had not been seen for two hundred years.

Those cheering signs and tokens for good, the pastor of Dun had eagerly watched from his quiet rural retreat; and it was with the exhilarating and hopeful feelings they inspired that he now came forth to enter on the second and more eventful half of his ministerial career.

CHAPTER V

1821–1830

PAROCHIAL WORK

———

Remembering without ceasing your work of faith, and labour of love, and patience of hope in our Lord Jesus Christ, in the sight of God and our Father.

—I THESS. i. 3.

TWELVE miles to the eastward of Glasgow, in the bosom of the long and fertile valley or strath which forms the line of the Forth and Clyde Canal, on a gentle rising ground at the foot of the Campsie Hills, which here soften down from rugged summits into an undulating line of quiet, green heights, stands the village of Kilsyth, with its busy mixed population of handloom weavers, colliers, and shopkeepers. The neat church and tower crowning the steepest acclivity of the hill looks out upon the strath to the west, and may be descried over its long level expanse as a white landmark for many a mile. The manse, with its sheltering thicket of planes and beeches, occupies another similar elevation at a quarter of a mile to the south, and commands an extensive and beautiful prospect, not only of the village and the hills, but down the long strath, level as the sea, to the far west. Even the blue summit of Goatfell, at the distance of sixty miles, can be seen from the parlour window in a clear day. The population of the parish was then 4,260, of whom 2,900 were in the town, and the rest landward. Such was the field of labour on which the subject of our sketch now entered, and which, as he looked out from his study window on the valley and the village, lay perpetually before his eyes, and as it were at his feet. The transition from the quiet rural scene he had just left was a great one. It was altogether a busier, noisier, livelier scene, in which he now found himself. Social life was at once more intense, more diversified, and more complicated. There was a greater stir of mind, greater variety of interests and excitements, greater impetus and force of existence every way,—intellectual, moral, social. The chatting groups in the market-place and the street corners,—the merry song often sustained in full chorus, blending with the sound of the shuttle in the long loom-shops,—the keen party politics, and the strong and even bitter denominational sympathies,— the eager and sometimes little-ceremonious canvassing of ministers and sermons,—the collisions and mutual jealousies between class and class, together with other manifestations of a more formidable and startling kind, peculiarly incident to the condition of large congregated masses, indicated a more active fermentation and vital play of all the elements of social life, and called from the new pastor a more strenuous bracing of himself, as for a new and more arduous task. In a religious point of view, the prospect, as it at first struck him, was at once discouraging and hopeful. There was at once more evil and more good in his new parish than in his former sphere. The powers alike of light and darkness were more awake, and the consequent collision and struggle keener. There was less negative respectability, but more of the positive fruits of grace. There was less profession, or rather, we might say, conformity to religious customs and observances, but more life. In the one case, the whole population were church-goers, while scarcely any were more; in the latter, a comparatively small proportion attended church, but among these a goodly number of decided and shining disciples, who were indeed lights of the world, and the salt of the earth. Instead, in short, of a uniform colour of decent mediocrity, the scene which now presented itself to him was that of a bright centre of living piety, surrounded by a dark shadow of open ungodliness and sin, stretching out on every side. The work before him was thus an arduous one; but in confronting it he found himself surrounded by a class of coadjutors such as before he had scarcely known—of ripe, experienced, intelligent, and prayerfully earnest Christians, who were ready to stand by his side, to cheer him on, and bear a helping hand in every good and holy work.

Still the tone of moral life in the place generally was very low. Intemperance was fearfully prevalent. Interwoven with all the immemorial customs and familiar incidents of daily life, it had grown into a kind of institution—an integral element in the existing social system. All ranks and classes were more or less infected by it.[1] Lairds, farmers, traders, weavers, colliers, artisans, were alike the patrons and too often, alas! the victims, of the tavern, which stared you face to face in every street and at every turn. On New Year days and fair days there was a regular carnival of wild excess, when a certain measure of indulgence, even on the part of those ordinarily decent and well-disposed, was reckoned rather a matter of course than as involving any stigma of reproach. All bargains and payments were settled over a "friendly glass" in the public-house; even the session-clerk met all applicants for proclamation and registration there, and became at last himself a victim of the insidious snare. At funerals, a strange ceremonial of blended prayers and potations was enacted—one round or "service" of the intoxicating

[1] To this there were of course many exceptions, conspicuous among whom was the chief heritor of the parish, Sir Archibald Edmonstone, of Duntreath, Bart., the faithful friend of the subject of this memoir from first to last, and, with his excellent lady, his powerful support in every plan and work of usefulness.

cup following another in solemn and imposing silence, with long and eloquent prayers interposed between, as if in the performance of some sacred libation for the dead. In this state of things it may well be conceived that the general tone of feeling and of public sentiment on the whole subject became sadly lowered. The minds of men were blunted by familiarity with the evil, and ceased to regard it with that abhorrence and shame which it deserved. It was singled out from other vices as a kind of venial sin—a soft weakness rather than a crime. Even the truly religious and well-disposed were not always sufficiently watchful against the danger, and large indulgence was extended even to some flaming professors, who prayed eloquently at funerals one day, and gave way to guilty excess the next. It will not be wondered at that this state of matters deeply impressed the mind of the new pastor, and gave a tone and direction to his views on the subject of intemperance which continued through life. He felt himself in front of a gigantic evil, against which it behoved him to summon all his strength, and, throwing away the scabbard, to fight manfully to the last.

Another characteristic feature of Kilsyth religious life very early and painfully struck him. This was the irregularity of attendance at public worship, which existed to a degree he had never before seen, and which thus seemed to him a peculiar habit of the place. It was not only that the number attending church was small in proportion to the population, but that the attendance of many of those who did come was fitful and uncertain. Those who were present in their places one Sabbath would absent themselves the next, without any cause or conceivable motive whatever. If the church was full for two Sabbaths in succession, it was more likely than otherwise to be visibly thinned on the third, however bright the sky and genial the season. On remarking this one day soon after his induction, to the factor for the chief heritor of the parish, "Oh!" said he, "that has always been the way here. The Apostle Paul himself could not bring the people of Kilsyth out in a full meeting three Sabbaths running." The proximate origin of this irregular habit, as given by the minister himself, as the result of a good deal of inquiry, is curious and instructive:—

"The parish church here had been long in bad repair,—a mean building at the best, and quite inadequate to the accommodation of the portion of the population, still a majority of the whole, who professedly adhered to the Established Church. At communion seasons, and through the summer months, worship had been conducted frequently in the open air. The consequence was, that the attendance had been irregular, and the pernicious habit of frequently absenting themselves from public worship fostered. Even after the long-deferred erection of a new church was set about, large allowance was made for the non-church-going habits, which had been much encouraged by the want of accommodation. The plan originally fixed upon had been curtailed, under the mistaken idea that the new church would always exhibit the pleasing spectacle of a well assembled congregation,—far more agreeable, certainly, than a vacuum. But the evil of irregular attendance, and the apology for it, were thus encouraged. …The great evil of *vacant* Sabbaths had also greatly tended in the same direction. During the ministry of Mr. Telfer, and, to a certain extent, during Dr. Rennie's, in the summer season there had frequently been no public worship in the parish church at all, the minister having been engaged at some neighbouring communion. The tent preaching, which was then universal in the west of Scotland, had given rise to this, and had made this particular evil unavoidable. No doubt, such seasons were blessed to many; but evil preponderated. Only a small part of the congregation could be supposed to travel a distance of five, six, or seven miles, to such gatherings. A large number were thus deprived of the benefits of public worship. The habit of irregular attendance was fostered. Those who had attended at these preachings were apt to satisfy themselves that they had laid in spiritual food for some weeks to come, and, without any cause, frequently remained at home. The cure of such an abuse as this, by the giving up of the tent, and by the regular provision of the ministrations of the sanctuary, along with the more frequent dispensation of the Lord's Supper, was unquestionably a great improvement. No doubt, some of the Lord's people, who got spiritual food at such solemn meetings, sighed after them; but it had been very generally agreed for some time that the change referred to had been very beneficial."

With such prospects, then, partly auspicious and partly adverse, Mr. Burns set himself to the working out of the problem before him with that quiet conscientiousness and calm steadfastness of purpose which, rather than any impetuous energy, distinguished him. As regarded himself, he was in the most favourable circumstances for girding himself for the great work of his life. He was in the very prime of life and the full maturity of his powers. Having persevered, too, during his twenty years' ministry in a retired rural parish, in the most regular and careful preparation of matter for the pulpit,[1] he was in possession of accumulated stores, which

[1] This good habit was certainly confirmed, though not originated, by an incident which happened soon after his settlement at Dun. On one occasion he had as usual prepared a careful sermon for the approaching Sabbath; but the day, when it came, proving so stormy as to promise only the skeleton of a congregation, he determined to reserve his elaborate discourse for another occasion, and in its stead to read a chapter, and make such free and familiar comments as he might be enabled at the time. He did so, and had advanced a certain way in the services, when, raising his head accidentally from the Bible, whom should he see straight before his face in the front gallery, but the distinguished Dugald Stewart, under whom he had studied some years before, and who, being on a visit in the neighbourhood, had made an effort to come and hear his old pupil! He proceeded, of course, with his exposition, as best he could, striving, doubtless, to realize the presence of a still greater Auditor, and thus overcome the fear of man, which bringeth a snare; but still, as he

enabled him now, without at all trenching on the full efficiency of his public appearances, to devote a comparatively large portion both of time and strength to the private duties of the pastoral care. To this work he from the first devoted himself with a persevering assiduity, which continued unabated to the last. Beginning his ministry with a general visitation and careful inspection of every family in the parish, he continued the same course year by year so long as strength remained to him, passing by only those whose strict connection with some other communion would have rendered such attentions invidious. Thus it might be truly said, that by the space of more than thirty continuous years, he ceased not to warn, to counsel, and instruct that people, keeping back nothing that was profitable, but "showing and teaching them the things of the kingdom of God, publicly and from house to house." It was not by any grand *coup de main*, or by a series of fitful, brilliant charges, that he expected to produce great results; but by a patient course of holy duty, continued on in faith and prayer from year to year. Thus his influence was rather felt than seen,—recognised in its slowly ripening results, rather than in the conspicuousness of the means. As time drew on, his plans and operations widened and multiplied. Adult classes for males and females were formed,—the Sabbath schools were organized, visited, watched over,—prayer-meetings,

---

used often to say, he resolved from that time "*never to preach a rainy day sermon again.*"

one or two of which had continued on, like the smouldering embers of a great fire, since the revival days of 1742, were fostered and multiplied,—a savings' bank was instituted,—a temperance society, headed by the minister and the parochial teacher, speedily followed,— a philosophical union, with its appropriate machinery of experiments and lectures, was originated. In all these schemes and undertakings the minister was either the prime mover or a zealous and efficient coadjutor, ever ready to bear a hand in any scheme which had for its object the physical, moral, or spiritual amelioration of the people, for whose good he was thinking and planning day by day.

Thus faithfully and unweariedly did he watch for souls as one that must give an account, instant in season and out of season,—becoming all things to all men, if by any means he might save some.

These efforts were not in vain. From a very early period in his ministry there were commencing tokens of that divine blessing on his work which towards its close became more and more conspicuous. Gradually though slowly the tone of moral and religious life in the congregation sensibly rose. Prevailing vices were abated. Reinforcements of intelligent and devoted members, the fruit chiefly of his Bible classes, were added to the eldership and the flock. The means of grace were more regularly and devoutly frequented. The spirit of prayer, and of wistful, expectant longing for better days,

increased. Thus the tide, which had been at the lowest
ebb, began sensibly to rise, and, creeping silently up the
shore, prepared the way for the great flood he was ere
long to see.

He was settled in Kilsyth, as we have said, in 1821.
In the year immediately following took place an event
which, though very trivial in itself, for the moment filled
all Scotland with delirious excitement,—the visit of
George IV. to his northern capital. As in duty bound,
the pastor of Kilsyth repaired to Edinburgh to pay his
homage to royalty. How he felt and demeaned himself
under this sudden blaze of majesty we do not know; but
the following itinerary notes of his homeward route will
be read with interest, as affording some fresh touches of
the every-day life of one immeasurably greater and more
kingly than George IV:—

"Upon the Saturday (the last during his majesty's
holding court among us), many ministers returned to
their various places of labour to perform their duties.
Among these were Dr. Chalmers, myself, and others,
amidst a great crowd, waiting to be carried on board the
steamer to Grangemouth. I met with the doctor and a
Glasgow gentleman, Mr. R— O—, waiting their turn
to be transferred to the already loaded vessel. In short,
we tired of waiting, and agreed to make a walking
expedition of it—to go to Bo'ness by the way of the
beautiful grounds of Dalmeny Park and of Hopetoun.
The doctor had made provision for his church in the

event of unexpected detention, and I had to preach at Polmont by exchange with my excellent friend Dr. Patrick Macfarlane, then minister there. The doctor had long promised to visit the manse of Bo'ness, Mrs. Rennie having been one of a family of his congregation, and much esteemed by the doctor; and Mr. O——, her brother, who was of our corps, encouraged the plan, it being his purpose to visit his sister at that time. The doctor and his friend set off, leaving me to follow so soon as my baggage could be disposed of. I did so with all convenient speed; but when I arrived at the eastern gate of Dalmeny Park, the keeper, in answer to my question if two gentlemen had passed there, told me that there were, but that his orders being not to admit any without some introduction, they had gone by the turnpike. He said that if I was known to any of the officials about the place, he would admit me: and I having mentioned the name of the factor in the city, who was my near relative, the gate was immediately thrown open. But what now of the doctor and his companion? At the Ha'as Inn at Queensferry I found them waiting. After being refreshed, I became cicerone in conducting them to the charming grounds of Hopetoun House, where royalty had lately breakfasted. By the way, speaking of Hopetoun House, I must give an anecdote of that nobleman and hero—the then Lord Hopetoun. His lordship was most exemplary in his devout attendance at church, both parts of the day. Having a shrewd suspicion one day that the domestics had the purpose of absenting themselves from public worship in the afternoon, he asked the butler why the servants were not preparing to move, when he told his lordship, that owing to some showers, and still drops falling, they were unwilling to wet their feet, or injure their clothes—in fact, were purposing to stay at home. Whereupon his lordship ordered out a commodious and ample conveyance for their transmission half a mile or less; and after learning from the butler that they were all seated and properly defended, his lordship took his large staff in his hand, and drove them all before him to church; after which they never afterwards thought of staying from the house of God on account of a shower or two. This brave and much-respected nobleman, having gone to the Continent shortly after the royal visit, was called away by a very sudden illness, far from his lovely domain! Returning, however, to our journey: The doctor was in a delightful mood; the day was fine (August month); the views to the north of the Firth enchanting. The large limestone rock on Lord Elgin's grounds, with the broad and gay streamer on the flag-staff crowning the elevation, was much admired, with a kind of chivalrous glow. Seated now and then, he looked round, expressing the delight which the scene and the occasion excited; for although in college days he was a good deal of the ardent Whig, and poured forth impassioned and eloquently-thrilling descriptions of the horrors of war, he was now, for a time at least, more of the Cavalier than the Round-head. On this subject we had some friendly argumentation. One time, on turning round and again expressing admiration of the flag on the lime rock, he said, 'What would a London Cockney say of this view? Well, it is after all a "neat concern."' Occasionally sauntering behind, he would pull a duo-decimo volume out of his pocket, and read a page of one of Owen's treatises, as food for the mind and heart, and then again join in conversation, both edifying and exhilarating. We then proceeded in our pedestrian course along the shore by Blackness, and had various talk of former scenes, while he, with his staff in hand, made good progress, saying that we had yet all the strength and buoyancy of our boyish days (I was now a year or two beyond forty—he about the same). ... The shades of evening were now upon us, as we entered Grange Pans—a pandemonian-looking place, difficult to penetrate even in daytime, but now doubly Cimmerian. We overtook a young sailor with very white trousers (the white trousers, in fact, served as a kind of torch to show us the way through the smoke of the salt pans), with whom Dr. Chalmers held converse. ... Next day Dr. Chalmers preached in Bo'ness church in the afternoon—his subject Rom. v. 10, 'If when ye were enemies ye were reconciled,' &c.—on the *a fortiori*[1]argument. This was quite an unexpected

---

[1] [Latin: literally "from the stronger (argument)". The term is used when drawing a conclusion that is even more obvious or convincing than the one just drawn.]

treat to the inhabitants of that small seaport. It reminded him of his beloved Anstruther, when he walked to the harbour and surveyed the opposite coast, Culross Abbey, and the adjacency."

It formed no small part of the charm of his new sphere of labour that it brought him to the neighbourhood of one whom he had known and admired in other days, while yet a great gulf separated them, and whose bright and burning course, after divine grace had touched his soul, he watched with peculiar interest and joy. The first time he heard this great man preach, after the great change had passed upon him—it was a public sermon at Glasgow for the sons of the clergy—he used often to speak of as an occasion never to be forgotten. The very tones of his voice as he read the opening psalm,—

> "Such pity as a father hath
> Unto his children dear,"

irresistibly touched him, and dwelt in tender cadence in his memory throughout all after years. He thought of the time when, as a student of divinity at St. Andrews, that same man had scouted the evangelical system as an obsolete tradition, and humorously advised my father to go out to Anstruther and see his parents, the only persons he knew who believed in such things,—and of another occasion still more vividly imprinted on the memory, when at an ordination in the Presbytery of Brechin he stood beside his old college friend, and, at the solemn moment of imposition, was in the act of thrusting out his riding-whip instead of his hand, whispering, "I suppose this will do equally well," when his more reverent companion held him back.[1] Such was Thomas Chalmers then and now—before and after that great moment in his history, from which and ever afterwards all old things were passed away, and all things were become new.

His connection with Glasgow, and with those eminent and faithful men who, from that time onwards, mustered stronger and stronger there, was the more precious to him, as at that period there were few of the country clergy round to whom he could look for congenial intercourse and profitable ministerial interchange. There is one only of our near neighbours of those days whose character and whole personality I vividly remember as deeply impressive. That was the venerable John Dempster, minister of Denny—a man alike in moral bearing and bodily stature stately and king-like, and whom all who were present at the convocation of 1842 must remember as perhaps the most striking figure in that assembly. Well do I remember, and even now see his lofty form as he came over the hill behind the manse on his tall chestnut horse, on which he sat erect and strong, like a knight-errant of former days. He was in the truest sense a man of

[1] This actually occurred at the ordination of an old college comrade, which he attended as a friend. My father used often to recur with a kind of reverential interest to the circumstance, as affording a vivid glimpse of the rude block out of which divine grace moulded so noble a form of Christian excellence and heroism.

God—an eloquent and even commanding preacher, too, when in his best vein, though rather fitful and unequal. His grand presence in the pulpit, and full majestic voice, was to us youngsters singularly impressive, and I hear to this hour the intonations of his voice repeating those words as his text on a communion Saturday, "Unto you that fear my name shall the Sun of righteousness arise with healing under his wings."[1]

But the great days at Kilsyth were undoubtedly those in which the sombre monotony of our rural preaching was disturbed by the louder and more stirring notes of the city pulpit. Dr. Patrick M'Farlane,[2] with his clear, pellucid flow of calm, chastened eloquence; Dr. Thomas Brown,[3] rolling along through prayer and sermon in a continuous stream of incandescent earnestness; and Dr.

---

[1] Besides Mr. Dempster, his most frequent assistants among his near neighbours were the Revs. Adam Foreman, of Kirkintilloch, a very worthy man of the old school, and John Watson, of Cumbernauld. At Campsie, there was, at the time of his settlement at Kilsyth, the too famous Mr. Lapslie, succeeded, however, afterwards by incumbents of a much higher cast. At Larbert, at a distance from Kilsyth of about eleven miles, was settled in 1826 Mr. John Bonar (now of the Free Church Colonial Committee), who soon came to be regarded as the very model of an able and faithful parish minister, and a very great accession to the cause of vital religion in that neighbourhood. Then, some years afterwards, came the bright and burning, but, alas! too brief ministry of the gifted and devoted John Brown Paterson, at Falkirk. Such, among the neighbouring clergy, were his chief associates and friends.

[2] Of the West Church, Greenock.

[3] Of St. John's, Glasgow.

Robert Burns,[1] the very embodiment itself of buoyant, bounding, triumphant energy, were our especial favourites, whose coming was ever esteemed an era—as a kind of avatar of the divine power and presence. That the visits of such men, and of others[2] of like spirit, whom my father ever gathered round him, were greatly blessed in preparing the way for better days, I have not the smallest doubt. Herein, doubtless, as in so many another instance, "was that saying true, One soweth and another reapeth; one man laboureth, and another entereth into his labours."

There is a pensive pleasure in thus recalling the visages and the voices of those who in long past days have spoken to us the word of life. I feel no delicacy in dwelling on what I know belongs not to us or to Kilsyth alone, but to all the world. Who is there among my readers who cannot set himself down in some quiet nook in some old church, and listen again and again to words which, spoken long ago to the outward ear, shall echo on in the heart for ever?

[1] Of St. George's, Paisley, now of Toronto.
[2] *E. g.*, Dr. John Smyth, of St. George's, Glasgow; Dr. John Forbes, of the Outer High; Dr. Henderson, of St. Enoch's, Glasgow, afterwards of the West Church, Greenock; and his old and cherished friend, and once more his near neighbour, Dr. Hamilton, of Strathblane.

CHAPTER VI

1821–1830

HOME LIFE

———————

Oh, how sweet that word! What beautiful and tender associations cluster thick around it! Compared with it, house, mansion, palace, are cold and heartless terms. But home! that word quickens the pulse, warms the heart, and stirs the soul to its depths, makes age feel young again, rouses apathy into energy, sustains the sailor on his midnight watch, inspires the soldier with courage on the field of battle, and imparts patient endurance to the worn-out sons of toil! The thought of it has proved a seven-fold shield to virtue; the very name of it has been a spell to call back the wanderer from the paths of vice; and far away where myrtles bloom and palm-trees wave, and the ocean sleeps upon coral strands, to the exile's fond fancy it clothes the naked rock, or stormy shore, or barren moor, or wild highland mountain, with charms he weeps to think of, and longs once more to see!

—THOMAS GUTHRIE

I N the midst of parochial and wider cares, the even current of the pastor's domestic life, at Kilsyth as at Dun, flowed tranquilly on. The stage had changed and the plot had somewhat thickened, but the drama and the actors were still the same. They had now six children besides the little one they had left quietly sleeping in that distant grave-yard—three sons and three daughters, of whom the eldest was now in his thirteenth year, and the youngest in her third. That, I imagine, must have been one of the happiest homes then on the earth. I daresay most children that have been nursed beneath the wings of parental love and prayer feel so, particularly, I think, those who have been reared in the country. There, where every house stands alone and apart from all others, with its own particular environment of wood and field and tree, which belongs to it, and to none other, the idea of home acquires a distinctness, a blessed isolation from all commoner and less sacred things which elsewhere it cannot have. Its whole surrounding circumstances, too, are more vivid, and crowd the young mind with those pictured images and scenes which in after years give charm and pathos to memory. The long, straight city streets, the sharp corners, and mathematical curves, make scarcely better pictures in the heart than on the canvas; while a single tree, or bush, or mossy stone, will live within the soul and before the mind's eye for ever. For this reason I have always thought those have suffered a great loss who have grown up from infancy to manhood in a city wilderness—something like the defect of a sense, or the want of an essential part of the complete education of the heart. The chambers of the memory in after life may indeed be airy and well-furnished, but certainly without pictures, or at least with very poor ones. The brook across which we leaped in childish days; the gnarled tree up which we clomb; the bright fields where we rollicked with the reapers or the hay-makers; the breezy wood in which we sported the live-long day amid the birds and the flowers; the bosky, winding dell which we explored with a kind of mysterious wonder reach after reach, till the trees became thin and scraggy, and we came out at last upon the still, upland heath or sheep-walk; the joyous days among the nuts or the brambles, or more joyous still, among the great snow-wreaths, when we could walk aloft over walls and hedges, and our house was blocked up from all the world, and the whole troop, exempt from school, turned out with spade and shovel to cut for ourselves a way; the misty loch, with its shifting crowds of curlers and skaters; the quiet walk to the house of God, with the grave-stones and the still groups around the door;—what man or woman reared in a country home does not know these things, and carry them evermore in the mind and heart as a kind of framing in of the dearest and holiest centre of his young life. In our case there was all this in fullest measure. A more distant expedition, too, now and then added incident and excitement to a scene which had otherwise been too still and unvaried. A fishing-party across the moorlands to Carron Water; a picnic in Campsie Glen; a journey *en famille* to Strathblane manse, the holiest and most blessed Christian home I ever knew; a glimpse of the great city, with its endless streets and forests of tall stalks towering up among the smoke; an excursion, one at a time, with father and mother to Paisley, or Borrowstownness, or Brechin, or Aberdeen, or St. Andrews;—these were the great events that vivified and diversified the even tenor of our ordinary domestic history. After all, however, it is the parent that makes the home; and surely in this respect ours was favoured beyond the lot of most. It was not that my father meddled much actively with the management of domestic affairs. His government was rather calm and strong than bustling and energetic. There was little direct systematic education. He was a regulating and steadying power, rather than a busy executive. He was, in short, felt rather as a presence than as an agency,—the element in which we lived, the atmosphere which we breathed day by day; something, in short, that was, as it were, presupposed, and in its silent influence entered into everything that was thought, felt, planned, enjoyed, or suffered within our little world. We were not often and much with him—not so much, I think, as would as a general thing be desirable. His calm and unimpulsive temperament here, as elsewhere, fitted him to act rather by continuous influence than by distinct and specific efforts. A casual rencounter in the garden-walk, or in the harvest-field; a forenoon drive to some neighbouring manse, or country-house; half an hour's private reading with his boys in the study before breakfast; above all, the Sabbath evening hour of catechising and prayer; these, with now and then the reading aloud in the fire-side circle of some interesting and popular volume—a task in which he greatly delighted and really excelled—were the chief occasions of direct intercourse between the father and the child. Sometimes, too, along the garden-walk at even-tide, or through a partition wall at midnight, the ejaculated words of secret meditation and prayer would reach our ears and hearts like the sounding of the high priest's bells within the vail.[1] The more active management of the household and of the home education was safe in the hands of his more nimble and lively partner, who seemed made, if any one ever was, to make home and home duties happy. Herself the very soul of springy activity and elastic cheerfulness, she kept all around her alive and stirring; while by the infection of her own blithesome and courageous spirit, labour became light and duty

---

[1] Such ejaculatory breathings of the quiet but fervent heart were peculiarly congenial to his calm and unimpulsive temperament, and became, as life advanced, more and more characteristic of him. Once, among the noisy crowd struggling around the door of the General Assembly, which had been suddenly shut for prayers, a deep voice was heard pronouncing the words, "The door was shut." It fell with a strange, solemn thrill on the ears of one who afterwards discovered that the speaker was the venerable pastor of Kilsyth.

pleasant. Never was she so much at home as when some sudden emergency in the house or in the fields summoned all hands to work, or when, in one of those occasional inundations of friendly kith and kin to which our large connection and central position[1] exposed us, the manse became too narrow for its inmates, and double-bedded rooms and extemporized shake-downs became the order of the day. Was there now and then, amid this universal quickness and alacrity, a slight tinge of sharpness in chiding the dreamy loiterer and the handless slut? Perhaps so; yet we children scarcely saw it, to whom she ever spoke in the true mother's tones of gentleness and love. From her lips and at her knee we learned our earliest lessons of truth, and in her voice and face first traced, as in a clear mirror, the lineaments of that gentle and loving godliness which hath the promise of the life that now is and of that which is to come. Yes, there she is, living,

[1] To the south of the manse, and within the bounds of the glebe, there is a gentle rising-ground, commanding from its summit an extensive prospect of the valley and of the line of the Forth and Clyde Canal, both to the east and west, and called by us, from this circumstance, "the Prospect." To this watch-tower we used to repair when visitors were expected, to catch the first gleam of the white passenger-boat as it turned a corner, or wormed its way through the over-shadowing trees in the far distance. But it would sometimes happen that, scarcely had the boat from the east deposited its freight, when that from the other quarter arrived with an unexpected contribution from the west, putting the resources and energy of the home office to the utmost possible strain without, however, producing a ministerial crisis, or any serious embarrassment which we youngsters could see.

life-like, just as we saw her thirty years ago sitting by the cradle side, rocking and singing her little one to rest; or in her own arm-chair, by the winter fire-side, with her happy group around her; or flitting and glimpsing like a thing of motion and light through the little household world that seemed to move in harmony to the tune of her light, quick step; or, as we saw her once on a sad and woeful time, pacing up and down with weary yet unwearying step during the long day and the long night with her dying darling in her arms,[1]—that poor, drooping one that would go to no arms but hers,—and then watching on to the last of those fearful breathings that shook the very couch, and sounded through every mother's chamber in the dwelling; or when, on some dark and stormy night, she tripped with light footsteps to our bedside when we were ill and fluttered with nameless terrors, and by her very look and voice chased all those fears away; or when we knelt at her feet and whispered our evening prayer; or surprised her in her closet, and found her on her knees; or on bright Sabbath days, when we all flocked around her to the house of God, and clustered about her in the family pew,—am I wrong in thus writing of one who still lingers with us, and who is

---

[1] This was our great domestic sorrow at Kilsyth—the death by croup of our youngest brother John, at the age of three years, on the 10th of May 1829. With his bright, rosy face and clustering golden locks, he was the idol of the family, as well as his mother's darling, when that fell disease, in those days baffling all medical skill, struck him down.

besides wholly unknown, even by name, to the outside world to whose indulgence we commit these lines? Yet it seems scarce possible to do full justice to the home life of the subject of our memoir, without saying this much of her who constituted to him so large a part of home, and of everything sacred and blessed associated with the name. At least I shall be pardoned, perhaps thanked, by many who remember with tears that they too had just such a mother, and how worthy of everlasting remembrance is that name that is recorded alone on the family Bible and on the church-yard stone. It is all over now,— that once happy home, with all its sacred endearments and joys, a thing of the past, existing only in memory and in dreams. Yet there is a solemn instruction as well as a pensive sweetness in reverting to it; and may none of those now so far scattered ever forget that they bear the responsibility as well as enjoy the blessing of having been reared in such a home, and followed throughout life's treacherous ways by such prayers!

CHAPTER VII

1830–1838

LONGINGS FOR REVIVAL

———

Awake, O north wind; and come, thou south; blow upon my garden, that the spices thereof may flow out.

—CANT. iv. 16.

THE subject of the revival of religion, as the great want of the times, had been brought under Mr. Burns's attention at a very early period, by the notices in Dr. Gillies's "Historical Collections" of the remarkable scenes at Kilsyth and Cambuslang in 1742-3, as well as by the brief but emphatic vindication of that work in Sir Henry Moncreiff's Life of Erskine. He had been brought even into immediate personal contact with a similar work of the Spirit in his own day, by some brief but cherished intercourse, in the year 1803, with the late lamented Dr. Stewart, of Moulin, and by a visit some years afterwards to the scene of his singularly successful ministry. Of that intercourse and that visit I am tempted to transcribe the following slight memoranda, as exhibiting one of the links in the chain of events to which we devote this chapter:—

"When a student at college I was familiar with the appearance of Dr. Alexander Stewart. About the period of his memorable letters to the pious Mr. David Black, of Lady Yester's, giving an account of his remarkable conversion, and of the revival in his parish, I saw him frequently in Lady Glenorchy's Chapel in the elders' seat (but not in the pulpit), where his sweet and placid, but serious countenance struck me much, and led to inquiry in regard to his history, which is so well known, and which is among the events which had a salutary effect on the state of religion in the Church.

"The Rev. C. Simeon's visit, along with the companion of his tour, James Haldane, was chiefly instrumental, by the divine blessing, in bringing about the wonderful and blessed change in his views and character, and which was followed with a marked and beneficial influence in that district—the scene of his then ministrations. In the notice of these memorable visits to Moulin, the biographer of Mr. Haldane has omitted to notice the excellent sister of Mr. Stewart, who was at that period his companion and housekeeper, through whom, I have understood, Mr. Simeon and Mr. Haldane were introduced to the manse of Moulin, and who had no small share in the interesting movement and meetings which followed. She was a person of superior intelligence, and was eminently helpful in the work. She was afterwards highly useful in a similar capacity in the manse of Cromarty,—combining the character of Martha and of Mary in managing the domestic concerns of that singularly interesting and original thinking man, whose early removal from this world still causes many a heart to thrill with affecting emotions.[1]

"With Dr. Stewart my acquaintanceship began in 1803, when he made a call upon my late brother of Brechin, to whom he kindly introduced himself, aware of the deep interest such men as he would take in the Moulin awakening. On a second visit he preached a forenoon in the church of Brechin, on the hosannahs of the multitude at our Lord's ascent to Jerusalem, with palm branches, &c. His manner was calm, and style of composition and of delivery tasteful and tender, not impetuous, or, in the ordinary sense, very striking or popular. His conversation in private was particularly

[1] Rev. Alexander Stewart, son of the above-named Dr. Stewart, of whom see a deeply interesting notice in Hugh Miller's "Schools and Schoolmasters," chap. xviii.: "I found on my return to Cromarty a new face in the pulpit. It was that of a remarkable man,—one of at once the most original thinkers and profound theologians I ever knew; though he has, alas! left as little mark of his exquisite talent behind him, as those sweet singers of former ages, the memory of whose enchanting notes has died, save as a doubtful echo, with the generation that heard them."—P. 391.

savoury, of a chastened character, reminding one of the expression of the Psalmist (Ps. cxxxi.), 'My soul is even as a weaned child.'

"In the year 1811, the year of a great comet, I had a solitary ride through Strathardle, Blair, Kenmore, &c. Having preached in the chapel of Persie (on the borders of two or three parishes), on the Monday I pursued my way on horseback by Kirkmichael in the above-named strath, on the way to Blair-Athol. I spent a night in Moulin. Several of the good people there, who had been quickened under Dr. Stewart's ministry, and who had come the whole way the day previous to the chapel in which I had officiated, waited on me at the inn, requesting an evening meeting for worship, and hearing the word. To avoid giving offence to the minister (now Dr. Duff, of Kenmore), whom I knew only by name, I did not formally call the people to a sermon, but to family worship in the largest room in the inn, when I expounded the word to a crowded meeting. I had a conversation with two very interesting men who had been elders in Mr. Stewart's time, and among the subjects of the gracious work there. They told me that they had paid a visit to their beloved spiritual father and former pastor, travelling the whole way on foot to Dingwall; and had a refreshing, though somewhat pensive meeting with one whose removal from among them they and so many deplored. One of these good men rose next morning and accompanied me on horseback for eight or ten miles by the beautiful seat of

Fascally, parting with me where the Moulin road joins the road from Dunkeld to Blair. I have seldom, if ever, met with a man of his station so interesting; his piety so humble and yet transparent, so full of love to the Saviour and to his cause. After much delightful Christian conversation, we parted, never to meet again in this world, but anticipating a blessed meeting in heaven, which is far better. I found unquestionable evidence, in my short visit to Moulin, of the reality of the far-famed revival in that district. I never met with Dr. Stewart after his removal to Dingwall."

And so the pastor went on his way, doubtless musing many things of the past and the future, and inwardly breathing such aspirations as that of the spouse— "Awake, O north wind; and come, thou south."

With such views and preparations of heart, it is not surprising that, on finding himself, in the providence of God, placed in the midst of one of the chief scenes of the former times of refreshing, the subject of revival became henceforth a ruling idea of his life. His public instructions, as well as private conversation at visitations and elsewhere, abounded with allusions to those happy days of the past, the remembrance of which had not yet wholly expired amongst the people, and with expressions of ardent longing for their return; and to this point might the whole course of his ministry be said more or less to turn. In 1822, the second year of his ministry, we find him, along with another congenial spirit, the humble and godly Dr. George Wright of Stirling, bending over the old records of the kirk-session bearing on the dates 1742-49, and with solemn interest decyphering the dim and fading lines that referred to the incidents of the work as then in progress. Towards the close of the same year (Dec. 1822), on two successive Sabbaths, he preached directly and fully on the subject, taking for his text those singularly appropriate and impressive words in Micah vii. 1—"Woe is me! for I am as when they have gathered the summer-fruits, as the grape-gleanings of the vintage: there is no cluster to eat; my soul desired the first ripe fruit"—bringing the whole case of past attainment and subsequent declension before the congregation, and calling upon them again to arise and seek the Lord. In 1830, in consequence of some unusual outbreaks of sin in connection with drunken brawls, a parochial day of fasting and prayer, in the view of prevailing sins and backslidings, was appointed by the kirk-session, and observed with marked seriousness and solemnity. In 1832 the near approach of the cholera, which fell heavily on the neighbouring village of Kirkintilloch, but never actually entered Kilsyth, while sounding its own terrible peal, at the same time summoned the pastor to lift up his voice in another earnest call to repentance and newness of life. In 1836 he read an elaborate essay before the clerical society in Glasgow, with the twofold object of calling more extensive attention to the subject, and of drawing forth the suggestions of the brethren in regard to some signs of awakening life that were even then appearing in his own parish. Such are some of the chief epochs in a course of action, and of holy longing, which, however, was incessant. The results of a more general kind in the improving tone of moral and religious life we have already noticed. By-and-by, tokens of a more specific character, distinctly foreshadowing a coming day of blessing, began to manifest themselves. There was a marked increase of seriousness and devout earnestness in public worship. The prayer-meetings were more and more thronged with wrestling supplicants and anxious seekers. One or two sermons at communion times, marked by a peculiar unction and power, had fallen with visibly solemnizing effect on the congregation, and stirred in secret many hearts.[1] Latterly, several remarkable conversions attested the still living power of the truth, and tended alike to startle the careless, and to animate and quicken the people of God.

One instance may be mentioned in particular as attended by circumstances peculiarly interesting and instructive. The head of a large family, in middle life, who had been marked hitherto rather by a mere heartless indifference than by any open acts of impiety or wickedness, had been repeatedly expostulated with by the minister for irregular attendance at the house of

---

[1] One in particular, by the Rev. A. N. Somerville, of Anderston, on the evening of a communion Sabbath, on the words, "Behold, I stand at the door and knock," will be vividly remembered by many.

God. Pleading the usual excuse of want of clothes, he had been now twice furnished with a full suit of decent attire; but after one or two Sabbaths' attendance he had again dropped out of sight, and the clothes mysteriously disappeared. The pastor's pleadings were renewed, and fresh promises of amendment made, provided the needful help was again vouchsafed. The matter was fully weighed and considered in the domestic council, and the result was, to make yet another trial before giving up the case as hopeless. The trial was made; the poor man was in his place with his family the next Sabbath; and, in that very first service, before the first prayer had closed, an arrow of divine conviction had pierced his soul, which the hand of the great Healer alone could extract. After a brief, but agonizing season of spiritual distress, he entered into perfect peace, and went on his way rejoicing. From that day he was a new man. His bright, beaming countenance, never to be missed at the hour of prayer from its place, became henceforth one of the chief ornaments of the sanctuary, while he was ever prominent among those who, in more secret assemblies, spoke often one to another, and wrestled, and waited for better days.

Thus already was the fallow ground turned up, and the soil prepared for the great seed-sowing and rich harvest that was near at hand. The fire was already kindled, and needed only a strong blast of the mighty rushing wind to rouse it into a flame. It was when matters were in this state, and when animated by those holy hopes and longings which these tokens of approaching blessing inspired, that the watchful pastor caught and improved an occasion which seemed to him eminently calculated to give an impulse to the good work. It was the anniversary of the death of the Rev. James Robe, who had been so eminently blessed in the revival scenes of the former century, and whose name still remained embalmed among the most sacred memories of the parish. He bethought himself of standing on the grave of that man of God, who, though dead, was yet speaking, and preaching on the words which had been inscribed by Robe himself in Hebrew letters over the dust of his deceased wife, "Thy dead men shall live, together with my dead body shall they arise. Awake and sing, ye that dwell in dust: for thy dew is as the dew of herbs, and the earth shall cast out the dead" (Isa. xxvi. 19). The occasion was a remarkably impressive and affecting one. It was a lovely, quiet Sabbath afternoon in August, and the romantic beauty of the spot, occupying the brow of the hill on which the manse stands, and commanding a full view of the valley, the village, and the surrounding hills, communicated a kind of picturesque solemnity to the scene. There, standing over the dust of his revered predecessor in the ministry, and surrounded by the children of that favoured flock to which he had ministered, and who now slept around him beneath their feet, he spoke in such earnest and weighty words as these:—[1]

---

[1] The extracts following are from the beginning and the close of

"You were previously aware, my friends, from what text I intended to address you this evening:—the words which have now been read in your hearing. They are inscribed in Hebrew characters upon the tombstone covering the mortal remains of the Rev. J. Robe, whose ministerial zeal and eminent success in the conversion of so many souls, especially in the years 1742 and 1743, has erected for him a monument more lasting by far than any reared by human hands, and formed of the most costly or durable materials. Eighty and four years have run their course since his mortal remains were laid in the dust close to the spot on which I now stand. Some of the usual emblems of mortality, and of the swift and imperceptible flight of time, are rudely sculptured on the stone:—the ship before the wind,—the quickly moving shuttle,— the hour glass of dry sand,—an opening grave,—and a trumpet sounding. But the words of our text, carved on the open volume,—the Bible,—express more plainly than any emblem or hieroglyphic the triumphant hope of the blessed, who have 'died in the Lord.' The letters on the tombstone are in a language to most of you altogether unknown, and they are already almost obliterated by the waste of time and of the elements of more than a hundred summers and winters.[1] But blessed be God, this text and the others referred to in explanation of the emblems are

the sermon, which will be found entire among the Remains in the second part of this volume.

[1] Mrs. Robe died in 1735, over whose dust this stone had been laid.

plainly legible in the blessed book which each of you possesses. What cause have we, my dear friends, to bless God that it is so,—that we need not spend our time in labouring to decypher characters becoming every year more obscure, and that the grand and blessed doctrine of salvation is not sealed up from you in a tongue known only to the learned, but made known in your native language—'Life and immortality brought to light by the gospel.' Job in early times—even as early as the times of Abraham—expressed his belief in the doctrine of the text, and wished his words to be written in a book, yea, to be graven on the rock, and, lo! it is fulfilled. They are in the faithful record, and more clearly and more fully known than if they had been literally committed to the memorial of the solid rock, the most impervious to the waste of time. Hear the profession of his faith and hope of a resurrection to life:—'I know that my Redeemer liveth, and that though after my skin worms destroy *this* body: yet in my flesh shall I see God, whom I shall see for myself, and not another, although my reins be consumed within me.' …

"My dear friends, the scene around us, and the occasion of our assembly this evening, are truly interesting and instructive. We are surrounded on all sides by the dust of friends and forefathers; where many of you worshipped in former times, and where often, often within walls[1] of which no fragment now remains, the

---

[1] Referring to the former church of Kilsyth, built in 1649, taken

memorials of your Redeemer's death were set forth, many a precious sermon delivered, and many a prayer poured out, and many a precious song of Zion sung. 'Our fathers! where are they?' The graves, and monumental stones, and inscriptions remind us that the people are grass, and that ministers are but earthen vessels. We surround the grave of one who was eminent in his day for zeal and success in the work of the Lord. He laboured in the vineyard for the long space of forty-one years, having been ordained in 1713, and departed this life in 1754. The narrative, well known amongst you, tells of the great things done in the latter years of his ministry, when many gave the best evidence of having been born again through the word then preached; and of vast assemblings along the adjoining stream, hearing with earnest hearts the words of life; and of the additional recurring sacramental seasons caused by the intense desire to enjoy such refreshing meetings. His memory is savoury. His sermons and 'Narrative,' and the holy character he maintained to the end, render his memory peculiarly precious. Two other ministers have subsequently laboured here, and have closed their ministry also. Their doctrine was the same as Mr. Robe's, although no such remarkable success attended their ministrations. And neither have we any new doctrine to publish, but have been humbly, and, we trust, sincerely preaching to you 'Christ Jesus, and him

---

down in 1816,—the new church being built in the village, and the romantic church-yard thus left as a solitary place of graves.

crucified.' Oh, will you not believe the gospel?—will you not embrace the faithful saying, and worthy of all acceptation, that Christ Jesus came into the world to save sinners, even the chief? Dearly beloved friends, the day is at hand when the hour-glass of time shall be emptied of its last grain,—when the trumpet shall sound, and the dead shall be raised,—when the bodies in this church-yard, now reduced to corruption and dust, shall awake, and all arise, either to glory and honour, or to shame and everlasting contempt. Oh, that the account we shall have to render may be with joy, and not with grief, for that would indeed be unprofitable for you! Blessed Jesus, the resurrection and the life,—who quickenest whom thou wilt,—by thy word and Spirit quicken us, and we will run after thee. Thou who calledst Lazarus to come forth, and immediately the dead arose, call the dead souls here to awake,—to arise a living army to praise thee; and oh, ere thou callest to judgment,—before the last trumpet sound, and the great white throne only be visible, and the Judge be seated on it,—while yet upon the throne of mercy, let poor, wretched, blind, and naked, fall down in humble, earnest petitioning for mercy and grace! Awake! O arm of the Lord, as in former times, as in days of old, 'Turn us, O Lord our God, and cause thy countenance to shine, and so we shall be saved!' Dearly beloved friends, when we part, after being in company together, whether in the market-place or in the house of God, we cannot be sure of ever all meeting again; but in the place of graves we shall meet, it may not be within *this church-yard*, but most certainly where all is equality—master and servant, great and small, parent and child, pastor and flock. Yet, there will be a separation. Ah, serious thought! there will be two congregations of the departed, who shall be on the right and on the left of the great Judge of all. Either, '*Depart, ye cursed*,' or, '*Come, ye blessed of my Father*,' will be addressed to each one of this assembly! Oh, to be numbered with the saints in glory everlasting,—to find mercy of the Lord in that day!"

Many afterwards spoke of this season as one by them never to be forgotten; and, but for the strong restraint with which the feelings of the hour were repressed, it has been thought that the outward manifestations of awakened life which arrested all eyes in the summer following might have dated from this day.

CHAPTER VIII

1839

LONGINGS FULFILLED

And it came to pass in the meanwhile, that the heaven was black with clouds and wind, and there was a great rain.—1 KINGS xviii. 45.

T HE following extract from a letter written by George Moody, Esq.,[1] writer, Paisley, son-in-law of Mr. Burns, to a sister in Edinburgh, will give a distinct idea of the state of matters in the parish towards the close of the year 1838. The writer, while a man of superior intelligence and information, was one of the most thorough and simple-hearted followers of Christ I ever knew, and was at this time pre-eminently one of those who "waited for the consolation of Israel." He was

---

[1] Brother of the Rev. A. Moody Stuart of St. Luke's, Edinburgh.

in the habit of residing during a part of the summer with his family at Croy Cottage, in the immediate neighbourhood of Kilsyth parish, and had thus the fullest opportunity of estimating the state of feeling, and of religious life there. The date is 5th September 1838:—

"There has been, and still is, a very pleasing work going on at Kilsyth, but you have been misinformed as to the extent of it. The accounts you have heard are altogether extravagant and exaggerated. But blessed be God there have been a few very marked and decided cases,—instances in which the hearts of careless, and even profligate and apparently abandoned sinners, have been subdued under the power of the truth, and to all appearance savingly enlightened and changed. The latest case is that of a man pretty well advanced in life, and the father of a grown-up family, a hearer in the parish church. He had been at one time very careless, and a drunkard, but within these few years became, along with many others, the subject of an outward change and reformation,—giving up his habit of dissipation, and becoming regular in his attendance at church, but at the same time giving no evidence of a regenerated heart. This state of things continued,—the man never dreaming that any further reformation was needed,—until a short time ago, when, witnessing the ordination of some elders in the church, one of whom was a great deal younger than himself, the thought struck him that there must be something far wrong with himself, when a person so much his inferior in point of years was considered fit to bear rule in the church, and he himself was conscious that he was not qualified for such an office. From that day he became unhappy, and his uneasiness became at last almost insupportable. He went to one of the numerous prayer-meetings in the village, and in the reading out and singing of the psalm his agony became so great that he shrieked aloud under the stingings of his wounded conscience. The little company joined in fervent prayer on his behalf; and their prayers were answered. The Spirit of grace spoke peace to his troubled soul, and he was enabled, feebly, indeed, but apparently in faith, to look to the Lamb of God which taketh away the sin of the world. From that day his comfort and joy increased, and he has been exhibiting all the fruits of an humble and renewed soul. Mr. and Mrs. Burns, from the conversations they have had with him, are both much satisfied of the reality of the work of grace in his heart. There are a good many instances equally, or nearly as remarkable, throughout the village; and there is, besides, a pretty general concern about spiritual things, increased attendance at prayer-meetings, at preachings, &c. In all this we have much cause of gratitude, and let us pray that the good work may go on and prosper, and be extended through the whole land."

Before these hopes and longings were fully realized, the gentle and loving heart that breathed them was still in death. Mr. Moody fell asleep in Jesus, after a very rapid decline, on the 11th July 1839, and was buried in the church-yard of the High Church, Paisley, of which he was a respected office-bearer, on Thursday the 18th July. His removal was not unconnected, at least as one of the lesser links in the divine chain of events, with the scenes which immediately thereafter followed. The day of the funeral was that also of our parochial fast, preparatory to the dispensation of the Lord's Supper, and my father, with the male members of the family then within reach, had of course to leave behind the solemn services of home, to take part in a work still more solemn. The circumstance was unusual, and communicated a deeper feeling of sacredness and awe to the errand which had thus summoned us away. Beside the grave there stood one whom God had been already preparing in secret for a great work, and who required only a final touch of the Master's hand to make him a polished shaft in his quiver.[1] The lowering down to the dust of one so dear to him, and the final closing of the earth over his head, till the restitution of all things, seemed to impart that touch, and he returned to the communion scenes at Kilsyth, in which he was to take part, with impressions and views of eternal things which communicated a peculiar earnestness and power to his words. My brother had been labouring for a short time in Dundee, in the congregation of the late lamented Mr. M'Cheyne, during his absence in the Holy Land, and had been doubtless much stirred and

---

[1] The Rev. William C. Burns, M.A., now missionary in China.

quickened in his own soul by his connection with a field which had been so richly watered and blessed. He brought with him, doubtless, from Dundee that hidden fire which at Paisley was roused into a flame. He preached first on the Saturday, in the district church of Banton, with such remarkable unction and power, that his uncle Dr. Robert Burns, who was present, insisted that he should take his place in the parish church at the evening service of the morrow. This he did, after much persuasion, and seeking of divine light, discoursing to a deeply riveted and solemnized audience on Matt. xi. 28,—"Come unto me," &c. From this moment he became manifestly the chief instrument in that deep movement and stirring of many hearts which had now fairly begun,—bravely leading the assault, for which his honoured parent had prepared the way by the patient siege of many years. The sequel of the history will be best told in the grave and simple words of the pastor himself, in a report which he gave in to the Presbytery of the bounds at the time, and which was, by their appointment, printed and widely circulated.

After briefly narrating some of the circumstances above adverted to, indicative of an approaching time of blessing, he proceeds as follows:—

"Still, after all these and other symptoms of good, it was not till Tuesday, the 23d July, that a decided and unquestionable religious revival took place. We may well say of the amazing scene we have witnessed, 'When the Lord turned our captivity we were as men that dreamed.'

We have, as it were, been awakened from a dream of a hundred years!

"The communion had been, as usual, upon the third Sabbath, and 21st day. Intimation had been made upon the Saturday, that the minister would wish to converse with such persons as were under religious concern, inasmuch as two or three had previously called upon that errand. The effect was that several other individuals did come to converse. The Monday evening was the half-yearly general meeting of our Missionary Society, when a sermon was delivered by Dr. Burns of Paisley—text, Isa. lii. 1: 'Awake,' &c. It was intimated that Mr. William C. Burns, who had preached several times with much power during the solemnity, would address the people of Kilsyth next day, if the weather proved favourable, in the open air; the object being to get those to hear the word who could not be brought out in the ordinary way. It was known, too, that he was very shortly to leave this place for Dundee, and probably soon to engage in missionary labours in a distant land. The day was cloudy and rainy. The crowd, however, in the Market Place was great; and on being invited to repair to the church, it was soon crowded to an overflow—the stairs, passages, and porches being filled with a large assemblage of all descriptions of persons, in their ordinary clothes. The prayer was solemn and affecting; the chapter read without any comment was Acts ii. The sermon proceeded from Ps. cx. 3, 'Thy people shall be willing in the day of thy power.'[1] Throughout the whole sermon there was more than usual seriousness and tenderness pervading the hearers; but it was towards the close, when depicting the remarkable scene at Kirk of Shotts, on the Monday after the communion there, 1630, when, under the preaching of Mr. John Livingstone, a native of Kilsyth, five hundred were converted, that the emotions of the audience became too strong to be suppressed. The eyes of most of the audience were in tears; and those who could observe the countenances of the hearers expected, half an hour before, the scene which followed. After reciting Mr. Livingstone's text, Ezek. xxxvi., 'A new heart will I give,' &c., and when pressing upon his hearers the all-important concern of salvation, while, with very uncommon pathos and tenderness, he pressed immediate acceptance of Christ, each for himself—when referring to the affecting and awful state in which he dreaded the thought of leaving so many of them whom he now saw probably for the last time—when, again and again, as he saw his words telling on the audience, beseeching sinners, old and young, to embrace Christ and be saved—when he was at the height of his appeal, with the words, '*No cross, no crown*,'—then it was that the emotions of the audience were most overpoweringly expressed. A scene which scarcely can be described took place. I have no doubt, from the effects which have followed, and from

[1] See notes of this sermon from the preacher's manuscript, in the Appendix.

the very numerous references to this day's service as the immediate cause of their remarkable change of heart and life, that the convincing and converting influence of the Holy Spirit was at that time most unusually and remarkably conveyed. For a time the preacher's voice was quite inaudible; a psalm was sung tremulously by the precentor, and by a portion of the audience, most of whom were in tears. I was called by one of the elders to come to a woman who was praying in deep distress; several individuals were removed to the session-house, and a prayer-meeting was immediately commenced. Dr. Burns of Paisley spoke to the people in church, in the way of caution and of direction, that the genuine, deep, inward working of the Spirit might go on, not encouraging animal excitement.

"The church was dismissed, after I had intimated that we were ready to converse with all who were distressed and anxious, and that there would be a meeting again in the evening for worship at six o'clock. We then adjourned to the vestry and session-house, which were completely filled with the spiritually afflicted, and a considerable time was occupied with them. Several of the distressed were relieved before we parted. These were persons believed to be Christians, but who were not before this rejoicing in hope. Others continued for days in great anxiety, and came again and again; but are now, generally speaking, in a peaceful and hopeful state, and have been conversing with a view to admission to the Lord's table.

"In the evening the church was again crowded to excess. Mr. Lyon, of Banton,[1] lectured on the parable of the prodigal son; and Mr. William C. Burns preached from Matt. xviii. 3, 'Except ye be converted,' &c. The impression was deepened; but there was no great excitement, the aim of the preacher being to forward a genuine work of the Spirit. A great many came to the manse to speak about their souls. Evening meetings in the church were continued without intermission, and even in the mornings occasionally. Our hands were full, but the work was precious, and often delightful. Our elders and praying men were, and still are, very useful in aiding us. He who was honoured as the chief instrument of the awakening was earnestly sought out, and our part in it became comparatively small till the work had made progress.

"On Thursday, the 25th, the day proving favourable, the meeting was called in the Market Square, where an immense crowd assembled at half-past six. From the top of a stair Mr. W. C. Burns addressed upwards of three thousand from Ps. lxxi. 16, 'I will go in the strength of the Lord God.' The emotions of the audience were powerful, but for the most part silent, though now and then there might be the utterance of feeling, and, in countenances beyond numbering, expressions of earnest and serious concern. Six young girls, from fourteen to sixteen years, two of them orphans, came next day bathed in tears, and

[1] Now of Broughty Ferry.

seeking Christ. The scene was deeply affecting. This day (26th) many conversations were held by Mr. W. C. Burns in the session-house; by myself and my other son (on trial for licence) in the manse. Upon Sabbath, the 28th, the church was crowded, and with the unusual appearance of not a few females without bonnets, and men and children in week-day and working dresses. I preached from Heb. iv. 16. In the afternoon we met at three, in the church-yard, where there assembled not fewer than four thousand. The sermon by Mr. W. C. Burns was solid and impressive, from Rom. viii. 1. He finished about five o'clock; but after the blessing was pronounced, about a third part either remained or soon returned, of various ages, but especially young; which led to various questionings at first, and then remarks, and appeals frequently repeated; which led to great meltings of heart in many, and in a few cases to considerable agitation; so much so, that my son and I continued to address the hearers in various ways, and to sing and pray over and over again, the people still unwilling to depart. Four of our pious men, two of whom were elders, were called to pray at intervals; which they did in a most appropriate and affecting manner. Even at half-past eight it was with difficulty we got to a close, proposing to have a meeting next morning at seven in the church. A great many still pressed around as we left the church-yard for the manse, and several remained till eleven or twelve o'clock. Next morning I went to the church at seven, after calling on an aged woman on the way, whose cries of distress arrested me. Even at that early hour there were from two to three hundred met in solemn silence, joining with me in prayer and praise, and listening to a short exposition of Song ii. 10-14. Through the whole day conversations were held in the manse, and in the vestry and session-house. In the evening the bell rang at half-past six. The church being before that filled, and as great a number pressing forward, it was found necessary to adjourn to the Market Square. Mr. Somerville, of Anderston, addressed a very large assembly of most attentive hearers, from John xvi. 14. At the close I was called to see three or four very affecting cases of mental distress, and there was still a desire to get more of the word and prayer. There was an adjournment to the church, where at first, as I understand (for I was engaged as above stated), there was considerable excitement, but which subsided into solemn and deep emotion, while Mr. W. C. Burns and Mr. Somerville addressed the people, and joined in prayer and praise. Next day at eleven A.M. Mr. Somerville again addressed a full congregation in the church.

"Ever since the date to which I have brought this imperfect narrative, with the exception of one evening, we have had meetings every evening for prayer, for the most part along with preaching of the word. On the evening referred to (the 6th August) there was held a meeting in the Relief Church, which was crowded by various classes, the work expressly approved of by the ministers present,—Mr. W. Anderson of Glasgow, and Mr. Banks of Paisley. From the first the people of the Relief congregation seemed interested in the work equally with our own people, and there appears to this day to be much of the spirit of love diffused among us. The state of society is completely changed. Politics are quite over with us. Religion is the only topic of interest. They who passed each other before, are now seen shaking hands, and conversing about the all-engrossing subject. The influence is so generally diffused, that a stranger going at hazard into any house would find himself in the midst of it.

"The awakening in the newly-erected parish of Banton has of late become most intensely interesting. At a prayer-meeting in the school there, the whole present, above one hundred men and women, not a few of them hardened miners and colliers, were melted. Every night since this day week there have been meetings in the church of Banton, and many earnest inquirers. The missionary, Mr. Lyon, whose labours have been for upwards of a year greatly blessed, has been aided, as I have been, by many excellent friends in the ministry, and the work goes on there in a manner fully as surprising as here. I am under obligations to my brethren for their ready and efficient services. I may just mention Mr. Duncan of Glasgow,[1] Mr. Macnaughtan of Paisley, Mr. Moody Stuart of

---

[1] Now Professor of Oriental languages in the New College, Edinburgh.

Edinburgh, Mr. M'Donald of Urquhart, Mr. Somerville of Anderston, and Mr. Jamieson Willis, as having been longest with us, and given valuable assistance; with Mr. Salmon, our former teacher.

"We are tried by the intrusion among us of teachers who are likely to sow divisions,—some of them, no doubt, much safer in doctrine than others. Strangers also who come among us, from good motives, are in danger of injuring our converts by over-kindness, and bringing them too much into notice. Enemies are waiting for occasion of triumph; and professors of religion, of a cold description, are doubting and waiting a long time ere they trust that any good is doing. Meantime the work proceeds most certainly; and from day to day there are additions to the 'Church of such as shall be saved.' The sermons preached are none of them eccentric or imaginative, but sound and scriptural; and there is not, as formerly, a tendency to compare the merits of preachers, but a hearing in earnest, and for life and death.

"The waiting on of young and older people at the close of each meeting, and the anxious asking of so many 'what to do'—the lively singing of the praises of God which every visitor remarks—the complete desuetude of swearing and foolish talking in our streets—the order and solemnity at all hours pervading—the song of praise and prayer almost in every house—the cessation of the tumults of the people—the consignment to the flames of volumes of infidelity and impurity[1]—the coming together for divine worship and heavenly teaching of such a multitude of our population day after day—the large catalogue of new intending communicants giving in their names, and conversing in the most interesting manner on the most important subjects—not a few of the old, careless sinners, and other frozen formalists, awakened, and made alive to God—the conversion of several poor colliers, who have come to me, and given the most satisfactory account of their change of mind and heart, are truly wonderful proofs of a most surprising and delightful revival.

"The case of D— S—, collier, may be mentioned as interesting. He had for some time been thoughtful, and had given up entirely taking any intoxicating liquor, and might be characterized as one of the more hopeful description. Since the present awakening, he was deeply convinced of his sin and misery, and for a month was deeply exercised, and spending much time in secret prayer and reading the Scriptures. On the evening of the 21st August, he had a meeting with several of his praying companions, and spent the night in prayer, praise, and converse. He appears to have obtained peace during that night, and came home to his house in a very happy state of mind. After taking two hours' rest, he worshipped

---

[1] "W— S—, in presence of an elder and several witnesses, with his own hand took down some books of this description, and put them in the fire."

with his family, and proceeded to his work. Being the foreman, it was his lot to descend first into the pit, which he did with unusual alacrity and with prayer. On reaching the bottom, the air instantly exploded, and in a moment he was ushered into eternity! How soothing and cheering the thought that he has escaped the everlasting burnings, and has passed literally through the fire to the regions of glory!

"But the bounds of this communication will not permit of enlargement. The work I consider as ongoing and increasing. The limits of Satan's domains here are diminishing daily. The accounts not a few give of their conversion is, that they could not think of being left a prey when others were making their escape. There is thus a provision made for the increase of the kingdom of Christ by a kind of laudable jealousy—a pressing in ere the door be shut.

"I have been engaged, and still continue to be engaged, in conversing with new communicants; and never before now have I had such pleasant work in listening to, and marking down, the accounts which the youngest to the oldest give of the state of their minds. While some, who seem to be savingly impressed, have given a somewhat *figurative* account of their feelings, yet, in by far the greater number of instances, they give most scriptural and intelligible accounts of their convictions, and of the grounds on which they rest their peace. Their experiences are evidently so various, as not to be in any degree copies of each other. Yet they all end in building upon the sure foundation, Christ in the promise, and Christ formed in them. The question naturally occurs, and has been put, 'Is there anything peculiar in the subjects and mode of address of the sermons which have been so remarkably successful?' I answer, that upon a groundwork of solid, clear, and simply-expressed views of divine truth, there was a great measure of affectionate, earnest pleading, a rich exhibition of the fulness and freeness of the gospel, eminently calculated to convey to the hearers the conviction and feeling of the sincerity of the preacher, and of the rich grace of the Lord Jesus. It has also been a matter of general remark, that there is an unction and deep solemnity in the *prayers* of the preacher who has been honoured to begin this work; and which, perhaps, even more than the sermons, have made way to the heart. We have had much precious truth presented to us by my much beloved brethren; to whom it must be gratifying to be assured, that, in conversations with my people, there have been references, I may say, to each of their discourses, as having been profitable as well as acceptable; and having been so well supported by their co-operation, and the Presbyterial notice taken of the subject, we cherish the pleasing hope that, under the special and continuing blessing of the great Head of the Church, this will prove not only a genuine, but an extensive and a permanent revival—the only means of arresting our downward course, and effecting that blessed consummation which the diffusion of merely intellectual knowledge will never accomplish.

* * *

"About three weeks after this remarkable work commenced, it was considered most desirable and obligatory to have *another* communion season. The Session met for special prayer for direction as to the matter, and afterward as to the *time* most suitable.

"The number of new communicants amounts to nearly ninety-nine. A few who spoke on the subject seem to have had scruples, and did not come forward. With the exception of a very few, the account given of their views and spiritual condition has been very pleasing and satisfying. They vary in regard to age from twelve to three score and ten; a good many are from fifteen to eighteen years of age. The work of examining has been of a different character from that of former years, wherein '*we have seen evil.*'[1] No doubt the systematic knowledge of not a few of them is deficient, and much pains must be taken by themselves and by us in this matter. I have urged on the young converts especially a very careful study of the Shorter Catechism, and the earnest, close, and prayerful study of the Scriptures. We solicit the prayers of Christian friends and ministers, that we may have the great joy of seeing our children 'walking in the truth,' and '*established with grace.*'

[1] See some touching entries on this subject in Journal quoted above, chap. iii.

"The number of communicants would doubtless have been greater had we deferred the communion for a few weeks, as the Banton revival is not so far advanced as to have furnished a large addition.

"A great concourse of people, including not a few genuine friends of the Lord Jesus, assembled to our communion. It is thought that not fewer than from twelve to fifteen thousand were *in and about* the town of Kilsyth upon the Lord's day; at the tent the number is estimated at about ten or twelve thousand. The day was uncommonly favourable; and, indeed, during the whole interesting season external circumstances were most propitious; and having been made the matter of special prayer, the answer should be marked and remembered.

"On the Fast-day (Thursday) public worship began at the usual hour, the minister commencing with praise and prayer, and reading Psalms cxxvi. and cxxx. The Rev. C. J. Brown of Edinburgh preached from Rom. vii. 9, 'I was alive without the law once,' &c. The Rev. Dr. Malan of Geneva preached in the afternoon from John xiv. 27, 'Peace I leave with you,' &c. Mr. Macnaughtan of Paisley preached in the evening, from Isa. xlii. 3, 'A bruised reed shall he not break,' &c. He preached also at Banton, and Mr. Cunningham of Edinburgh[1] from the words in Rom. v. 8, 'God *commendeth his love* toward us.' Friday evening the Rev. Mr. Middleton of Strathmiglo preached from Jer. viii. 22, 'Is there no balm in Gilead;

---

[1] Now Principal Cunningham, of New College, Edinburgh.

is there no physician there?' Saturday, Mr. W. C. Burns preached in the tent to a large assembly from Rom. x. 4, 'Christ is the end of the law,' &c. In the evening Mr. Somerville of Anderston preached to a crowded audience from John xvi., on the work of the Spirit. This was a remarkable night of prayer, secret and social; probably there was not an hour or watch of the night altogether silent. The beds were not much occupied; many, like the Psalmist, prevented the dawning of the morning. The morning bell rung at nine o'clock, and worship began at fully twenty minutes to ten, both in church and at the tent. The action sermon was from John vi. 35, 'I am the bread of life,' &c. Mr. Brown of Edinburgh fenced the tables. Mr. Rose of Glasgow preached in the tent and fenced the tables.

"The first table, as usual, contained about one hundred; but to prevent confusion and undue protraction of the services, arising from so unusual a number of communicants, the second was composed of those already seated in the body of the church; after this the third was composed of those in the usual bounds, with a few seats additional; and the remainder were served in the usual tables: so that the great accession was not felt as any obstruction to order or comfort. The ministers were at full liberty to address the communicants without the constant urgency of studied brevity. There were eight services, as follows:—The minister, first; Mr. Martin of Bathgate, second; Mr. Dempster of Denny, third; Mr.

Brown, fourth; Mr. Somerville, fifth; Mr. Rose, sixth; Mr. Duncan, Kirkintilloch, seventh; and Dr. Dewar, eighth.

"Mr. Rose preached in the evening from Isa. xlii. 3. All over by nine, without interval. In the tent, after Mr. Rose, Mr. W. C. Burns, Mr. Middleton, Mr. Somerville, and Dr. Dewar preached. Mr. W. C. Burns preached again, by moonlight, to a great assembly, from 'The mountains may depart,' &c. All was most orderly and decorous, and in many cases there were symptoms of deep emotion. We have heard of several well-authenticated cases of persons who came with levity of mind and went away deeply impressed; and of one or two who *could not get away*, but remained over Monday. Besides the vast crowd at the tent, Messrs. Martin, Dempster, Brown, and Harper (of Bannockburn) severally addressed a group of people near the church, waiting for entrance to the tables.[1] After public service, a great number of the godly strangers, and of our young members, and of persons concerned about salvation, remained. The younger ministers present continued in exhortation, prayer, and psalms successively, for a considerable time, in a most solemn, affectionate manner, feeling unusual enlargement in their own spirits, with much of the felt gracious presence of God.

"On Monday, at a quarter past eleven, probably from two to three thousand assembled around the tent.[2] Dr.

[1] "The communion proceeded in the ordinary way in the Relief Church, with the assistance of Mr. Frew from St. Ninian's."

[2] "Many ministers were present that day. Besides those already

Dewar preached from John xvi. 8, ' He (the Spirit of truth) will convince the world of sin,' &c. Mr. W. C. Burns preached from Ezek. xxxvi. 23-26, 'A new heart will I give you,' &c. The hour of five struck ere all was over, and very few withdrew previously. The sensation was deep and solemn. In the evening Mr. Brown preached in the church, from 'What do ye more than others?' Similar exercises were engaged in also on the Monday night as on Sabbath night; which the ungodly jeer at, the formal wonder at and censure, and which many good Christians would at first pronounce rather carrying it too far. But the fact is, that this is a spring-tide, a very uncommon season, in which a rigid adherence to the rules of ordinary times must not be applied. We have been drawing up a large draught, and the nets cannot be kept and laid by so orderly and silently as usual.

"This precious season of communion is now over and gone, but the remembrance is sweet. Having been preceded, accompanied, and followed by a very unusual

---

mentioned we noticed Mr. Laurie of Gargunnock; Mr. Leitch, Stirling; Mr. Hetherington of Torphichen; Mr. Cochran, Cumbernauld; Mr. J. Willis; Mr. Bonar, and Mr. Morison of Larbert; and Mr. Jaffray, Paisley. Mr. Lee of Campsie was present upon Saturday; and on the Sabbath, Mr. Forman of Kirkintilloch and Mr. Cochran. Many excellent elders also were present assisting us, as Mr. R. Brown, Fairlie; Dr. Russell, Edinburgh; Mr. R. Moody; Mr. H. Knox; Mr. John Robertson; Mr. Islay Burns; Mr. Penney, Glasgow; Mr. Simpson, Port-Glasgow; Mr. M'Donald, Cochno; Bailie Shaw, Rutherglen; Bailie M'Kenzie, Inverness; Captain Hay, Fairlie; Mr. M'Allester, Paisley; Captain Haldane; and Allan Buchanan, Glasgow."

copiousness of prayer, the showers in answer have been very copious and refreshing. We are daily hearing of good done to strangers, who came Zaccheus-like to see what it was, who have been pierced in heart and have gone away new men. Our own people of Christian spirit have been greatly enlivened and strengthened, and some very hopeful cases of apparently real beginnings of new life have been brought to our knowledge. I feel grateful to the God of grace and God of order in the churches, that there has been such a concurrence of what is true, *venerable*, pure, just, lovely, and of good report, and that little indeed has escaped from any of us which can justly cause regret. We are anxious (we trust we have a good conscience) that nothing should be done against, but everything *for* the truth, that God in all things may be glorified through Jesus Christ. The solemn appearance of the communion tables, and the delightful manner in which they were exhorted—the presence of not a few unusually *young* disciples at the tables—the seriousness of aspect in all, and the softening and melting look of others, made upon every rightly disposed witness a very delightful impression. May the Lord give abundant increase.

"For ninety years, doubtless, there has not been in this parish such a season of prayer and holy communings and conferences—nor at any period such a number of precious sermons delivered. The spiritual awakenings and the genuine conversions at this time are not few, and it is hoped will come forth to victory; but the annals of eternity only will divulge the whole! The *enemy*, the devil, has been also among us, and is doubtless busy *now*—more so than at the time of this dispensation. We are not ignorant of his devices.

"Yet, upon the whole, there is much cause indeed to give God the glory for what he has wrought. That he hath been the chief worker is most undoubted; for 'the Son of God was manifested to destroy the works of the devil,' and his works have been much damaged and brought down among us. The public-houses, the coal-pits,[1] the harvest reaping fields, the weaving loom-steads, the recesses of our glens, and the sequestered haughs around, all may be called to witness, that there is a mighty change in this place for the better.

"The wicked scoff—nay, some we hear around us, or passing by, have brought upon themselves the great guilt of speaking evil of this work. We pray for them. 'They know not what they do!' Some decent professors and moral people are opposed to this whole work, and say, 'If it continue it may do good;' but they do nothing to make it continue, and others throw cold water upon it. It is strange, that when sermons seem to make no impression,

[1] "A coal master here bears witness, that the colliers, who were formerly drunk ten days in the month, are now sober, and that instead of swearing, they have prayer-meetings below ground, and are orderly. And why should colliers not be numbered among saints, and be kings and priests to God? Pious colliers and minors, what a treasure!"

these persons should feel no anxiety about the permanency of the good expected; but when there is really appearance of good impressions, their doubt should be expressed about the duration of the good promised. Shall we be satisfied that we preach, and are heard, and no one showing any concern, but just sitting, and, it may be, sleeping out the hours, and returning home as they came? Surely, surely, even a degree, yea, a great deal of enthusiasm, is better than death-like insensibility.

"Such godly fear has come upon the people, that scarcely a single instance of intoxication, or any approach to it, has been observed in the whole multitude assembled, whereas formerly the prevalence of this and the quarrels it engendered, brought dishonour on tent-preaching, and in fact extinguished it.

"Special instances of good done are naturally called for. Many memorable cases can be produced. Selection is difficult. A woman from Airdrie was observed by a few around her to be much impressed while Mr. W. C. Burns preached. She at length left the field and retired for prayer. After a little she was followed by some praying people, who conversed with her. She seems to have undergone a complete change, and went away in a composed frame. A young gentleman from Glasgow, with whom I and Mr. Brown conversed, who had come with some indefinite notion of good or of being pleased, went home a new man in Christ Jesus.

"I add a very few words in the way of inference.

"1*st*, Prayer united, as well as secret, for the bestowal of the Spirit's influence, is most important, and will sooner or later be heard.

"2*d*, *Extra* means should be used to bring those *without the pale* of any church to hear the gospel. The preaching of the former summer in the church-yard once and again, and the late frequent addresses in the market and field, have most certainly brought the word near to many who might have remained to their dying day without hearing it. Assuredly these means must be used, otherwise our newly provided churches will remain unoccupied, and in a great degree useless.

"3*d*, There is a close connection betwixt *missionary* work and revivals. Our newly organized missionary society, in January this year, has been marked by several people as an era. No Church can be in a lively state when nothing is done for the heathen.

"4*th*, The social nature of man is an important element in his constitution, and exerts a powerful influence on the state of the Church and of the world. There are those who view the weavers' shops as objects of unmingled aversion, as hotbeds of anarchy; but when a good influence is made to bear upon the minds of the operatives, the facilities for *good* are proportional to those for evil—the reviving interest spreads much quicker than in a rural district. Let every minister of the gospel, and every Christian patriot keep this steadily in view and ply the workshops with every good and generous influence.

Never let us cease, in good times and bad, to essay to do good, in the morning sowing seed, and in the evening withholding not our hand; thus are we to sow beside all waters. God give the increase!

The movement thus begun quickly spread during the months that followed to other places at a greater or a less distance from the sphere of its first manifestation. At Dundee, at Perth, at Aberdeen, in the glens and straths of Aberfeldy and Blair-Athol, and far away in the Highlands of Ross-shire, the scenes of Kilsyth were, with slightly varying circumstances, renewed, and many souls were quickened from the dead, and many more baptized with new life and power from on high. In other places where no such remarkable outward manifestations occurred, the breathings of the same Spirit were in gentler and more silent, but not less real influence experienced. Many a pastoral vineyard in which faith and prayer had toiled for years in vain, were during those blessed months bathed in soft, refreshing dew. Individual souls, too, who from far distances and from many different parishes, had found their way to some of the great centres of the work, especially at communion times, carried with them on their return to their respective homes the sacred impressions they had received; while many ministers who had either taken part in the services, or were present as worshippers and witnesses, returned to their own flocks to preach the old words of life with new unction and power. Thus from the bosom of those great fires which the divine Spirit had kindled here and there over the land, were thousands of burning sparks cast forth on every side around, and many a live coal earned away to kindle other fires elsewhere.[1] Even the mere rumour

---

[1] Of this wider influence, the following extract from a letter addressed to the author by a devoted, and eminently judicious minister in the neighbourhood of Glasgow (Mr. Munro of Rutherglen), may serve as an illustration. Testimonies of the same kind might be multiplied indefinitely:—

"I regret to say my recollection of the influence of the wonderful work of God at Kilsyth in '39 begins to grow dusky. I know, however, that a very considerable number of my people visited the place, where the 'Lord appeared so signally in his glory building up Zion,'—and some of these repeatedly, as I had the blessed privilege of doing myself. Moreover, I distinctly remember that a very unusual solemnity and spiritual concern manifested themselves, and for a period of many weeks, more or less generally over my congregation, in connection with personal visits made to Kilsyth, and the loud-voiced rehearsal of the Lord's glorious doings there. Further, and finally, I have good reason to believe that several individuals were at Kilsyth translated from the power of darkness into the kingdom of God,—of whom one is now in glory, one in America, and one still with me—reduced, alas! by epilepsy to the borders of idiocy,—a deeply interesting case, for the worthy creature has long and deservedly borne the soubriquet of the *Poor Man's Minister*; and a greater number, I am persuaded, were most sensibly quickened and revived, of whom one is with the Lord. He was a native of Kilsyth, but had long been settled here as a physician. I think he must have seen three score years and ten, when he visited his birthplace, and returned rejoicing in God as he certainly had never done before, and that joy remained until, as I believe, it became full in the land of uprightness. Another of those last specified is a most exemplary elder of Free St. —'s, where he has been severely tried by remarkable worldly prosperity. He was in '39 a poor, infirm young man, and now he is both able and willing of his

and spreading fame of those stately marchings of the King of Zion were not without its important influence on the Church at large. The minds of men were powerfully drawn to the subject of the Spirit's work, and familiarized, at least, with the idea of far greater things to be done by His presence and power than had been known or dreamt of in their day. The whole tone of feeling and conviction throughout the Christian community in regard to such matters was heightened, and hopes and longings kindled in thousands of hearts for a glorious coming development of the kingdom of God, which are now at last finding their fulfilment. Certain it is, that from the hour that these remarkable scenes at Kilsyth and Dundee became generally known throughout the land, the idea of revival as the great necessity of the Church and of the age,—till then but a dim tradition of bygone days,—took strong possession of the minds of Christian men, and has never since lost its hold. From that hour it ceased to seem to them a thing incredible that God should raise the dead; nor have there ever since been wanting among them select souls who have watched and waited before the tomb of a dead Church and of a dead world, in the sure and certain hope of a mighty shaking and a glorious resurrection ere long.

Thus, even in the order of cause and effect, the events of 1839 and those of the present hour are not unconnected.

substance, as well as otherwise, to help the Lord against the mighty. And there is an eminently godly man of frail health, but burning zeal in the cause of Christ."

The earlier season of blessing was not only the precursor, but in a sense also the preparation for, and the pioneer of, the other. The one stirred up the hopes and awoke the suppliant longings which the other is fulfilling. Who can tell, for instance, to what an extent the vast circulation of such books as the Memoir and Remains of the saintly M'Cheyne, with its brief but stirring notices of the revival scenes amid which he lived and moved, may have, through the divine blessing, contributed both to prepare the soil and scatter wide the seed for the great harvest we now behold? In itself, however, the former movement was comparatively local and partial. It was confined, at least in its marked and conspicuous manifestations, to a few favoured spots, and followed chiefly in the track of a few peculiarly gifted and powerfully awakening evangelists. It was but a passing, though precious vernal shower, in prelude and earnest of those more plenteous rains and floods upon the dry ground that were ere long to come.

CHAPTER IX

1839–1859

FRUITS AND RESULTS

The kingdom of heaven is like unto a net, that was cast into the sea, and gathered of every kind; which, when it was full, they drew to shore, and gathered the good into vessels, but cast the bad away.—MATT. xiii. 47, 48.

MORE than twenty years have now elapsed since those solemn scenes, which have been described, transpired. There has thus been ample time for fully testing the reality and the permanency of the work then accomplished. What has been the result of that trial? What stamp has Time, the judge of final appeal in all such questions, set upon a movement then so generally welcomed and hailed by the godly, but so variously judged by the outer world? The question is one which, in any case relevant and interesting, has acquired a largely enhanced importance from the events of recent years. When scenes like those at Kilsyth are renewed on so many fields and over so wide an extent of the Christian Church, when a long, broad wave of spiritual influence and impression, compared with which the movement of 1839 was but a partial and local swell of the tide, seems rolling round the world, it becomes a matter of the utmost urgency to determine what was, in point of fact, the full and final issue of the former work— the result of the problem as it now stands, as matter of history worked out and complete? To this question I have heard many answers—some of them sufficiently decisive and sweeping, by those living far from the spot, and enjoying but scanty means for forming a calm and deliberate judgment. Some one living near the place and occasionally visiting it, has, with little or no inquiry, passed a disparaging judgment; and others, at a greater distance, have repeated and proclaimed it as if a final settlement of the whole question. "The whole thing," it is said, "has passed away." "Like a baseless vision it has vanished, leaving not a rack behind." "A mere fit of passing excitement, resulting in a re-action of deeper carelessness than ever." "I know the place very well, and have visited it often, and can testify that it is, as it always was, one of the most wicked and unruly towns of the west country." To these allegations, which I regret to find have become pretty extensively disseminated over the country, a few sentences may be offered by way of reply. I may state at the outset, that the above most certainly was not the impression of the subject of this memoir, than whom surely none were better entitled and qualified to pronounce an authoritative judgment. Having lived and moved in the very midst of the work from first to last, and watched its course and results most narrowly day by day for nearly twenty years, had it indeed proved the entire failure which some have represented, and evaporated in mere smoke, he must have known it, and mourned therein the wreck of all his most ardent hopes and prayers. It was not so. The fact is, that he lived and died in the full and unclouded conviction that the movement of 1839, or rather, the movement which reached its crisis and culminating point in 1839, was a genuine and most blessed work of the Spirit of God, and had been proved so, not more by its first promise and blossom, than by its after and enduring results. To have given forth this testimony at large in a permanent form to the world, was to the last one of the most cherished desires of his life; and for this purpose he had made extensive, though unfortunately incomplete, preparations some years before his death. That desire can never now be realized; but I feel that I am only reporting his dying testimony, and executing as far as is now possible his last legacy to the Church, by thus expressing in brief what in the copious memoranda and corroborative documents before me lies recorded at length. That amid so many hundred souls that were at first touched with divine impressions, many went back and walked no more with Christ; that some enlisted apparently under the banner of the cross, and yet gave back in the day of battle; that tares sprang up among the wheat; that the crowded and laden net gathered of every kind, both bad and good, is of course true, and, however sad, is surely not strange; but it is equally true that many then awakened to newness of life, or baptized afresh with the Spirit of grace, have continued steadfast in their holy profession, and have either already finished their course with joy, or remain to adorn the doctrine of God their Saviour in the world. The fire that was then, as we believe, brought down from above, still burns on the altar of many hearts, and will, we doubt not, burn on to the end.

That Kilsyth still is—now as before—a very wicked place, or, at least, in this respect very like other villages of the same size and character, is, I daresay, quite true. When was it that Christianity or the Christian Church ever by its influence permanently pervaded, and regenerated, and transformed the world? It is not in the world, but in the people whom it gathers out of the world that its vivifying and new-creating power is fully seen. It is now as it has ever been, when the True Light has shone in a fresh epiphany on the world. "He was in the world, but the world knew him not; he came unto his own, and his own received him not; but as many as received him, to them he gave power to become the sons of God, even to them that believe on his name, which were born, not of blood, nor of the will of the flesh, nor of the will of man, but of God." That there have been in that parish many happy souls thus spirit-born, and who have manifested this their heavenly birth by shining, like their Master, as lights in the darkness, is simply matter of fact, and surely more than this was not to be expected. The time, no doubt, is coming when not only shall the Church be revived and enlarged, but the world renewed,—when the handful of leaven shall not only ferment and work its way within, but pervade the whole lump—but not now. I suppose the visible effects produced by Christianity in the days of its first triumphs on the general tone of society in the great centres of its influence was not great. We have no reason to believe that in such communities as Ephesus, and Corinth, and Rome, the whole face of things palpable to an observer's eye was changed,—that those cities of the world were visibly transformed into cities of God. I suspect an intelligent and shrewd observer might have passed through Corinth, and even lived in it for weeks, during the very time of St. Paul's ministry there, and yet never have seen, or heard, or suspected that anything extraordinary had taken place, or was going on there. He would find the streets, doubtless, as gay as ever,—society in all its relations as foully corrupt,—the tone of public sentiment and feeling as frivolous and godless. I wonder if some twenty years after St. Paul's coming there, "to Corinthianize" had ceased to be the expressive title for the life of those who to the fullest measure fulfilled the desires of the flesh and of the mind? There is at least no trace of any such transformation in any records of that time that have come down to us. On the contrary, the whole Roman world, and the entire frame of society then existing, went on, as all history testifies, corrupting, and inwardly rotting more and more, until in the end it was, not regenerated and renewed, but swept away and buried out of sight. The Church was not so much the restorer of the old society as itself a new and nobler society rising out of the ruins of the old,—the ark that rose aloft above the universal wreck, and bore in its bosom the germs of another and better order of things. That besides this, and even at the time, it exercised, by its very presence, a certain salutary influence on the relations of social life beyond the circle of its own immediate pale, we need not doubt; but that influence at the best was slight and partial, and was of no avail whatever to arrest the tide of general corruption and licentiousness which had long before set in, and was now rushing on to its highest flood. And such, more or less, is its history in every nation and every community to which it comes. It is the salt of the earth, conserving and purifying so far, but only so far, as its influence spreads,—the light of the world, shining in, but not necessarily dissipating, the darkness. In the instance now in question, indeed, it might have seemed at the time to a sanguine observer as if it were to be more. At the first outbreak of holy impression, it seemed as if the influence were universal. The hearts of thousands were simultaneously stirred with spiritual concern, and a solemn awe and fear pervaded the community. There were inquirers, more or less anxious, in every street,— almost, as it seemed, in every second house. Iniquity, as ashamed, hid its face; sinners in Zion became afraid, and the one thing needful became on all hands the one absorbing subject of thought and converse. Loom-shops were turned into places of prayer, and factories into preaching stations. The church was thronged night after night for months together with eager and earnest worshippers, while prayer-meetings, like water runnels swollen by winter rains, teemed and overflowed on every side. This, of course, did not last. Surface impressions died away; convictions that had not issued in conversion were quickly quenched; the sudden panic passed; and scared but untouched hearts began to recover their self-possession, and breathe freely again. The host of the enemy had been for the moment utterly broken and scattered, as if in total rout; but by-and-by they began to rally and close their lines anew. The great blaze of holy fire that had all at once burst forth, died gradually down, and only those coals that had been thoroughly ignited continued to burn on. But these did burn on; many of them, as I have already said, until this hour.[1]

[1] These remarks, made in the first instance in regard to Kilsyth, apply equally to the other scenes of the revival movement referred to at the close of the last chapter. Thus I learn from the Rev. John Milne of St. Leonard's, Perth, with whose congregation the awakening

Other circumstances, too, contribute, in course of time, to efface the more patent traces of such a movement as this. The composition of the community itself is perpetually changing. The death or removal to other places of old residents, and the influx of strangers,—whether gradually, or, as it happened in the case of Kilsyth, in a sudden inundation,[1]—soon imparts an entirely new complexion to society, so that, though it is still the same place, it is no longer the same people. The old race passes away, and a new generation, bred under other influences, and blended with other elements, rises up in their place. Thus the congregation and village community of today is at best the descendant only, rather than the continuation and actual representative of the revived Church and parish of twenty years ago. A solitary door here and there in each street, a solitary name here and there in the communion roll, represent all that now remain of that old people on whom two-thirds of a generation have already done their work, and which is now mainly a harvest reaped down and gathered in. Yet even still enough remains on the spot to convince

---

in that city was chiefly connected, that not only did a very large proportion of the original subjects of the revival continue steadfast, and hold on in the ever-brightening path of the just, but that new cases of decided conversion appeared from time to time for years afterwards, the first germs of which were distinctly traceable to the awakening shock of these solemn days.

[1] Consisting of a large colony of navvies in connection with the Edinburgh and Glasgow Railway works.

the devout and candid inquirer that it is indeed a field which the Lord hath blessed,—that the work there done by his right hand was indeed honourable and glorious, and well worthy of being sought out by all those that have pleasure therein.

CHAPTER X

1843–1859

DISRUPTION TIMES AND CLOSING SCENES

If any man will come after me, let him deny himself, and take up his cross, and follow me.—MATT. xvi. 24.

THE times of refreshing we have just described were speedily followed by times of trial. The baptism of grace was the preparation for a baptism of temptation and of suffering. Thus, within three years of the period of which we have been speaking, we find the venerable subject of these lines appending his name, with the other fathers of the Church, to the invitation which called together the Convocation of 1842; and in the year following he sat as a member in the memorable Disruption Assembly, and formed one of the hoary band which gave a kind of picturesque dignity and pathos to the solemn procession from St. Andrew's Church to Canonmills. Thus he had by his life, as it were, bridged over the great gulf between the zero Assembly of 1796, and the culminating Assembly of 1843,—witnessing the one as a student and spectator, and taking part in the great work of the other as an honoured confessor and martyr. His views on the great questions then at stake were moderate, but decided,—strong, but not extreme. While with many others of his revered fathers and brethren he would have been prepared cheerfully to acquiesce in the veto, or the Duke of Argyle's bill as a practical settlement of the non-intrusion question for many years to come, on the vital issue of the Church's spiritual independence and her sole responsibility in matters sacred to her divine Head and King, he was resolute and immovable. So when the moment of trial came, his decision was instant and unhesitating. Without a murmur he laid his earthly all at the feet of that Master whose cause, as he believed, demanded the sacrifice, and signed the irrevocable deed of renunciation with firm and unshaking hand.

But it was not without a struggle that he could tear himself away from those altars at which he had ministered for more than forty years, and turn his back for ever on the sanctuary he had loved so well, and with which all the holiest joys and sorrows of his life had been bound up. Trying scenes were yet before him ere the formal deed of the hand could become a realized and consummated fact in the life. He must not only lay his sacrifice on the altar, but with his own hand he must slay it, and offer it up before the Lord. After all, it was not at Canonmills, amid that enthusiastic and applauding assembly, but at the closed manse door and the churchyard stile, that the true sacrifice of faith and patience was made,—there that those brave hearts that had forsaken all for Christ received their sharpest and deepest wound. How many a parochial and domestic tragedy of deepest pathos was, during those few succeeding days, enacted far away among the valleys and hills, that will never find a record on earth, but which, if recorded, would form a history more thrilling far than that even of solemn convocations and enthusiastic assemblies, "the day" alone will declare. It was the disruption only of the ecclesiastical constitution that took place at Edinburgh; the disruption of the Church,—of the real, living body, member from member, nerve from nerve,—the rending asunder of the living heart-strings took place elsewhere. The following simple incidents may be taken as a specimen of the kind of scenes which make up the annals of that unwritten history. During my father's absence at Edinburgh, the removal of the family from the manse to another and humbler dwelling in the village had been already accomplished; but having left town rather sooner than was expected, he returned home in ignorance of the fact. Landing in the dusk of evening by the canal boat, the instinct of old habit carried him to the door of the now deserted mansion. He knocked once—twice—thrice, waking the hollow echoes louder and louder. At last the close-barred shutters, and the silent and deserted look of the place flashed upon his mind the real state of the case, and he awoke up as from a dream. Turning away, his eye caught the dim forms of two men standing at a little distance in intent, and apparently interested observation. They were two of his attached parishioners, who, seeing him turn in this way, and comprehending at once the whole state of the case, had followed their pastor's steps, and had stood watching the scene with deep emotion. They grasped his hand in fervent sympathy and congratulation. Thus he turned his back for ever on the endeared home of so many happy years. The Sabbath following he held the service in the church-yard. There was no worship in the parish church, so that his old congregation still assembled round him undivided. He addressed them on the solemn and appropriate words, "The time is come that judgment must begin at the house of God; and if it first begin at us, what shall the end be of them that obey not the gospel of God?" The Sabbath following was looked forward to with still deeper anxiety. It had been rumoured during the week that the parish church would on that day be re-opened, without fail, for divine service, and the disruption of the congregation accordingly was inevitable. My father spoke little about this, but evidently thought and felt much. It had been arranged that morning service should be held at an early hour in the Relief Church, the use of which had been kindly offered by the minister and congregation, and that thereafter another meeting should be held, should the weather prove favourable, in the open air at the usual hour of worship. The first service was over, and the minister had gone with some members of his family to the house of a respected elder close by, to perform a baptism. While the solemn rite was proceeding, the well-known tones of the parish church bell were heard tolling for divine service. The quick eye of one who had been his companion for well nigh forty years was instinctively turned to the pastor's face, and marked it first suddenly flush, then turn deadly pale. The service went on and closed; nothing was said of what was still on the mind and heart of all; and the minister, taking hold of the venerable elder's arm, and leaning on it heavily, proceeded in silence to the place of meeting. A great concourse was gathered on a beautiful grassy slope close beneath the parish church, and bounded on its lower verge by a little pebbly stream. The rumoured service in the church had proved a false alarm, and the few that had assembled there, after waiting a short time, slowly dispersed, or dropped in one by one into the larger assembly below. So his old parish flock met yet again around him unbroken. There was a pause of deathly silence as the congregation, now assembled and seated, waited the arrival of their aged pastor, for whom, in this the hour of his sorest trial, many hearts were lifted up in prayer. He appeared at last from a neighbouring cottage, preceded by the Bible and Psalm-book, advancing with his grey, uncovered head to the place prepared for him. The people, as I have often heard since, scarce venturing to look up, were rather conscious of his presence than actually cognizant of it, and a deep, suppressed groan passed like a chill shudder through the assembly. Many said afterwards that they could not dare to look up to his face till the opening psalm and first prayer were over. But his own soul, after the first struggle, was buoyant and strong, and he preached with more than usual unction and comfort on those grand words, "Thanks be unto God, who always causeth us to triumph in Christ, making manifest the savour of his knowledge by us in every place." The morning had been at first cloudy and uncertain, but as the day advanced the sun shone out in glory, and the evening closed in beauty and in peace. It was a cheering omen for the future. Sabbath after Sabbath, for months together, did that congregation, and hundreds of others over the length and breadth of Scotland, in quiet valleys, on bleak hill sides, and on naked shores, meet for worship under the open canopy of heaven; and it has been often remarked, that during all that time there was scarcely one rainy, or even showery Sabbath. Thus did their gracious Lord, whom they owned and worshipped as Head over all things for his Church, order even those lesser things for their good, "staying his rough wind in the day of his east wind." By-and-by things settled down into their ordinary course. The exalted excitement of that great epoch gave place to the more flat and calm routine of common life. A new church and manse, reared by the hands of a willing people, rose up in the room of those he had left behind, and his old flock, but little thinned by the fiery ordeal they had passed through, rallied strongly round him. Pastoral work was resumed, old plans of usefulness renewed with the freshness of feeling and the new impulse which change of circumstance inspired. At home, in the bosom of his flock, and in the work he loved, he cast sometimes a pensive, but never a lingering look to the goodly heritage he had left behind. The step he had taken, with all its sharpness of suffering and sorrow, he had taken deliberately, and without the shadow of a doubt as to the path of duty, and he never regretted it. His last manse, he used often to say cheerfully, was, after all, thanks to the generous toils of his friend Dr. Guthrie, the best and most commodious he had ever tenanted. The most bitter drop in the cup, doubtless, must have been the sight day by day of his own successor in that office and station which he had never thought to quit but with life; but soon that, too, became familiar to him, and imparted only to his spirit a touch of chastened sadness, in which there was not the least tinge of bitterness. The chief change perceptible in the daily course of his thoughts and feelings was, that they were more congregational and less parochial. In former days he had identified himself almost with the very soil of his allotted vineyard, and every hill and dale within its measured bounds had been dear to him. Well do I remember, often when on our homeward route from some distant expedition, we crossed the narrow brook that formed the boundary line of our own parish, how his spirits would rise, and he would remark with a blithe smile again and again, what a "bonny" parish it was; nor would he ever on such occasions admit its inferiority to any scenes of beauty we had seen in our way. Now it was not so much the parish, as the flock in which he garnered up his heart. Years flowed on. The infirmities of age were stealing upon him, but seemed for long to touch him very gently. His eye remained undimmed, and natural strength unabated, while he gradually passed from green to ripe old age, and the reverend father became the hoary patriarch of the parish and the country side. Even when the heavier hand of time visibly impaired his physical powers, his heart was still young, and his mind clear as ever. The old habits of reading and study were pursued sedulously, and he had a fresh eye and heart for all that was going on in the Church and in the world around him. So he held on his way, growing stronger and younger, as it seemed, in spirit, as his bodily life gently ebbed away, pursuing, as ever, his quiet, accustomed round of pastoral diligence and activity, and still in his old ejaculatory way of musing soliloquy, singing like a happy husbandman at his work, and casting the frequent upward glance to the great Master:—"Shine forth from between the cherubims." "O send out thy light and thy truth." "Walked on Sir A. Edmonstone's new private road musing on subjects of discourse. Heard a bell ring at the quarry. Thought with myself, what does this mean? It is a signal to drop work, being Saturday. One of the workmen said to me, You had better move, as there is to be an explosion of gunpowder. I was not tardy in making away. Thus a warning may be disregarded through ignorance and want of thought. I might have understood the signal, but did not,—was dreaming and loitering, but a friendly voice roused me. How many, alas! thus linger and delay, though danger is near, and though often loudly warned! Education begins not with the alphabet. It begins with a mother's look and a father's nod of approbation, or sigh of reproof,—with a sister's gentle pressure of the hand, or a brother's noble act of kindness. We have it in the flowers, and in the green-daisied meadows; the birds' nests admired, but not touched; in pleasant walks, in kindly salutations, in acts of benevolence, in deeds of virtue, in the source of all good, in God himself." "Read 'Olney Hymns,'—sweet preparation for prayer" (Eph. vi. 10). "Before rising, gave glory to God; much cause. I will sing. We will sing of mercy and of judgment. Unto thee, O Lord, will we sing. O come unto us!" "Day very stormy, as the night was. Read at worship 65th Psalm, and 50th. Offer unto God thanksgiving. Resumed study; prayed for preachers and all preparing for tomorrow. O for preparation! to get the word digested in my own mind and heart, and then may it flow out for the benefit of all, and produce golden fruit!" "Visited Robert Burns's daughter, Mary. I fear a dying child—very promising. The mother much afflicted. Walked a little on the green and burnside—all hoary (1st Jan. 1850). A funeral from B— came up. How soon we have mementoes! Ere this jubilee year be over how many will be below the green sod! My induction having been at the close of the year, 4th of December 1800, eleven months yet to run ere the fiftieth year. How solemn the thought of nearing that which is so rarely reached!" Such are the fragments of musing thought and heavenward breathing which I find scattered over every page of his brief daily memoranda of this period, and which were ever and anon, too, dropping from his lips in solitary reverie, as a kind of accompaniment to the more active business of his life, like the hum of the busy bee, or the "quiet tune" with which the lowly brook murmurs on its way. On the 4th of December 1850, he completed the fiftieth year of his ministry. A public meeting was proposed to him by his people in celebration of the event, but he declined an ovation, in which he feared much fulsome and vain-glorious flattery would mingle, preferring a private and unobtrusive presentation, amid Christian converse and prayer, of a handsome testimonial of affectionate respect, which his people had prepared for him. He was now in his last decade of life. He was baptizing day by day the children of those who had been themselves baptized by his hand in the commencing days of his ministry. The representative and almost the sole survivor of one generation, he was gently welcoming another to the place and the work they had left behind. Soon he too will be going home. A few years more, during which his well-known form was still seen in pastoral round, or amid the homes of the sick and dying, and his sun went down with the calm brightness of the man whose path is as the shining light, shining more and more unto the perfect day.

CHAPTER XI

APRIL AND MAY, 1859

THE LAST ENEMY

———

Sun of my soul! thou Saviour dear,
It is not night if thou be near;
Oh! may no earth-born cloud arise
To hide thee from thy servant's eyes.
Abide with me from morn till eve,
For without thee I cannot live:
Abide with me when night is nigh,
For without thee I dare not die.
　　　　　　　　　—CHRISTIAN YEAR

THOUGH for several years his strength had
been perceptibly declining, and a colleague
and successor[1] had been associated with him

---

[1] The Rev. Robert Black, now sole pastor of the congregation.

in the pastoral charge of his flock, it was not till about a year before his last illness that any decided signs of approaching dissolution appeared. During a visit to his children at Cupar-Angus and Dundee, in April 1858, the central organ of nourishment refused to do its office, and the effect was soon seen in his sadly altered face and form, on which the signatures of death seemed already written. Reaching home, however, he rallied wonderfully, and enjoyed during the winter months that followed a considerable measure of his wonted health and spirits. But in spring the old symptoms returned with increased severity, and with every token of a fatal issue. Still he did not himself at first look upon this as his last illness. His breathing was so free, his pulse so regular and full, every organ and member so sound and unimpaired, save only the one failing function whose ailments we are accustomed to regard as amongst the lesser maladies of life, that he could scarcely realize that the whole mechanism was going to dissolution and decay. At last, however, the real state of the case was made known to him. He received the tidings with surprise, but with cheerful welcome, and from that moment calmly prepared for his end. The following particulars of the closing scene are from notes made at the time by my valued brother-in-law, the Rev. Thomas Bain of Cupar-Angus, who was with the beloved sufferer almost uninterruptedly to the last, and by his unwearied ministrations both to the soul and the body, was indeed more to him than a son:—

"The Rev. Dr. Burns ended his life of abundant labours and eminent usefulness at the Free Manse of Kilsyth, on the morning of Sabbath, the 8th day of May 1859, at ten minutes before five o'clock. A few recollections of his last interesting and instructive sayings are here recorded by one who enjoyed the great privilege of ministering to his temporal comfort during the few closing days of his life.

"The weakness which at last laid low his massive and once robust and active frame, commenced about ten weeks before his death; this weakness gradually increased till he was able to sit up, only for a few hours at a time. The last day of his public service on earth was Sabbath, 27th March, when he preached from the text, 'A faithful man who can find?' He was scarcely able to ascend the pulpit; but as there was no supply forthcoming for that day, by a very great effort he engaged in his loved employment, and was wonderfully strengthened during the first part of the service, but found after praise and prayer that he was unable to finish the discourse. Many of the people felt or feared it was his last appearance in that pulpit, where, till the advanced age of eighty, which he reached two months before, he had continued to break the bread of life amongst his people, most of whom he had baptized and admitted to the communion of the Church, and many of whom, there is reason to believe, he had been the honoured instrument of guiding to the Saviour. On leaving the church many of the congregation were observed deeply affected by this consideration. After that

Sabbath he was confined chiefly to the house, and in a great measure to his bed.

"The testimony borne by him, during his last illness, to the faithfulness of his covenant God, and the power of his all-efficacious grace was in full accordance with a long life of usefulness in his master's service. He was, we believe, the father of the Free Church of Scotland, having reached the very advanced period of fifty-nine years of active service as an ordained minister of Christ, and enjoying such vigour and health during all that period, that, as he remarked to several friends, he had only been prevented on two Sabbaths by ill health from preaching the gospel of the grace of God, and scarcely ever complaining even of a headache till within the last two or three hours of his life. Some of his remarks on his death-bed were deeply affecting, and the scene was one never to be forgotten by those who witnessed it. Praise and prayer had for many years been the exercises in which he found the chief delight, and his love for singing the praises of his heavenly Father was very remarkably manifested during his last illness; his favourite hymns were frequently read to him and sung at his own request, such as—

"'Begone unbelief,'   …   …   *Newton.*

"'When troubles assail,'…   …   *Newton.*

"'When languor and disease,' …   *Toplady.*

"'There is a land of pure delight,' …   *Watts.*

"'O tell me no more,' …	…	*Gambold.*
"'I lay my sins on Jesus,' …	…	*Bonar.*
"'Children of the heavenly King,' …		*Cennick.*

"This last was sung at his own express desire an hour before his death.

"Dr. Rainy, from Glasgow, came to see him on Thursday, 5th May, by which time his strength had been very greatly reduced; Dr. Burns was not aware that Dr. Rainy had been requested to visit him, and on his entering his sick room, he raised himself, and with great energy said, 'How kind, my beloved friend, to come and see me; how wonderful that all friends are so kind to me, a poor unworthy creature, when many of the Lord's dear children, and the Lord himself, had few to show them kindness!'

"His constitution was so good, and his lungs so sound, that he did not fully realize till a few days before his death that his end was drawing nigh. 'If I only could get something to restore the tone of my stomach,' he one day said, 'I think I might still wear through this attack,' having had a similar one about the same season last year. 'Ah no, father,' said his daughter, 'this is the battle with the last enemy.' 'Do you think so?' said he, calmly and even cheerfully. 'Oh yes,' it was replied. 'And does the doctor think so?' 'Oh yes, he does.' 'I am very glad of it,' said he; and after that he scarce had one other thought about life. He had a desire to remain for the sake of his poor flock, who lay very near his heart; but he had a stronger desire still to depart and to be with Christ, which was far better. After he had fully realized that his end was approaching, his meekness, and humility, and longing to be with Christ were very beautifully displayed in harmony together. His frequent exclamation was, 'Let me away! Lord, take me home!' During severe sickness, which was one of the most distressing aspects of his illness, he was heard praying, 'Father, didst thou not promise to deliver? I have sought three things; one of them I have got. Oh, give now the victory over the last enemy!' And, on another occasion, when suffering very great distress from the same cause, his ejaculations were, 'Lord, thou canst not refuse me,' and after a pause, 'for *His* sake.' The singing of his favourite psalms and hymns always soothed him, even when he was in the greatest suffering; and when it was thought he was realizing little of the world without, even till within one hour of his end, he was often heard joining with his low bass voice in the last line or words of the verse, and always adding in a loud, clear voice, *'Amen, Amen.'*

"When means were tried to alleviate his suffering, and he was revived from the deathlike sickness which often oppressed him, his exclamation again and again was, 'I cannot come back; I am going, I am going; I am willing, I am willing; Lord, *come, come, come.*'

"Having rallied from one of his very severe attacks of sickness, he was unusually cheerful, taking hold of the hand of one of his sons, another son and a son-in-law standing by, he said, 'How kind you all are! how wonderfully the Lord orders all things! I used,' added he, 'to boast of my age, thinking, when I was fourscore, I am quite well; the Lord is now teaching me the truth of his word,—*labour and sorrow.*' When refreshed with water during sickness, his constant word was, 'Blessed water, streams from Lebanon.'

"After singing, at his own request, 'The hour of my departure's come,' he said, 'Now no more—leave me— let me go—don't touch me.'

"This verse he often desired to be repeated to him, and was observed listening with deep interest and feeling to the following verse, 'Not in mine innocence I trust;' though innocence, as far as it could be found in fallen man, was one of the peculiar features of his character.

"During the slight wandering of his mind, which till very near the close had been very acute, his expressions were still in the same strain,—

"'Is there no way of fainting away? Oh, let me faint and get home; Lord Jesus receive me to thyself; there is room enough for me;' and then throwing off the clothes with his arms extended, he cried with a loud voice, 'Open to me the gates of righteousness!'—his attitude and expression of countenance reminding us of David's words, 'Oh, that I had wings like a dove, that I might fly away and be at rest.'

"When some of the family, who resided at a distance, were trying to comfort him with those words of consolation with which he had often comforted others, he said, 'We have been too little together, we have had too little fellowship; but there will be uninterrupted fellowship above. Oh, for more of the Spirit! Blessed Spirit! *enrich, enrich.*' He never once expressed a doubt or fear about his acceptance, but was longing to get home. He at times, however, mourned over his coldness, 'Blessed Jesus,' said he, 'how have I offended thee! Why is my heart so cold?'

"The last hours of his life were employed in ejaculatory prayer, and dwelling on the promises of the word of life. Late on Saturday evening we asked him what psalm he would like us to sing. After a moment's consideration he said, 'Sixteenth, two last verses, "*Thou wilt not leave my soul in hell—Thou wilt me show the path of life*,"' and after singing them he mentioned the fortieth. We then prayed beside his bed, and his loud and hearty '*Amen*' closed the prayer. After a pause he said, 'Return unto thy rest, O my soul, for the Lord hath dealt bountifully with thee,'—'close with that,' he said. We wondered if he knew it was Saturday night; he evidently was aware of it, for after singing that, he supposed the Sabbath had come, though it was a few hours before twelve o'clock, and said, 'Now let all be assembled to be addressed,' and when no service was begun, he said, 'Will ye no do it, the work of eight days is too much for me.' He was a good deal excited after this, but his language was that of triumph and peace. '*I die in peace*—I am willing—into thine hand I commit my spirit; thou hast redeemed me, O Lord God of truth. I desire to depart'—to be with Christ, it was added; 'Yes—and I will see his face, and I will behold his glory—*glory—glory—glory!* Come, come away—I hear his voice—let me go. Thanks, thanks be to God who giveth us the victory—thanks to God for his unspeakable gift. We will conclude,' he said, still imagining it was the Sabbath service; 'in dwellings of the righteous is heard the melody of joy and health.'

"Sabbath morning at length was reached, that day he loved so well. We had a strong impression the day of his entering on his rest above would be the blessed Sabbath of rest below. A hard conflict with the king of terrors was gone through during the early hours of Sabbath morning, during which he was heard praying, 'Didst thou not promise to give thy beloved sleep? Lord, give thy beloved sleep;' and then taking up the language of triumph again, he said, 'My Beloved is mine, and I am his—that's long ago.' One of his last expressions was, 'Into thine hands I commend my spirit,' adding with peculiar emphasis, 'for thou *hast* redeemed me, O Lord God of truth,' and then quietly and gently he said, 'All's well.'"

It was at this time, about three quarters of an hour before his death, that he asked us to join him in singing the hymn:—

> "Children of the heavenly King,
>   As ye journey sweetly sing;

> Sing your Saviour's worthy praise,
> Glorious in his works and ways.
>
> Ye are travelling home to God,
> In the way the fathers trod;
> They are happy now—and ye
> Soon their happiness shall see.
>
> Shout, ye ransomed flock, and blest,
> Ye on Jesus' throne shall rest;
> There your seat is now prepared,
> There your kingdom and reward.
>
> Fear not, brethren, joyful stand
> On the borders of your land;
> Jesus Christ, God's only son.
> Bids you undismayed go on.
>
> Lord, obediently we'll go,
> Gladly leaving all below;
> Only thou our leader be,
> And we still will follow thee."

As we sung these words in full chorus, though with faltering voice, he listened earnestly, and audibly joined in the last line of several of the verses. That was his swan's song.

"His last message to his family standing around was, '*Children*,' repeating the word frequently, and with difficulty getting the remainder of the verse out, but dwelling earnestly on it, 'Children of the light, and not of the darkness—walk as children of the light—children of the light—children of the light.'

"After this life gradually ebbed away—the breathing getting weaker and weaker, till he fell asleep in Jesus, and lay with a calm placidity of expression, which told that all anxiety, and care, and suffering were over, and that the ransomed spirit had been caught up to join the songs of Zion above.

"'Blessed are the dead who die in the Lord, from henceforth. Yea, saith the Spirit, they rest from their labours, and their works do follow them.'

"The record of the works which shall follow our beloved father, the great day of accounts will declare."

The grey dawn of the Sabbath morning was stealing gently in when the great silence of the death-moment fell upon us. The world without was just awaking, and the birds sang cheerily among the branches, just as they had done, at the birth of each succeeding day, for six thousand years, and as they will do, amid all the vicissitudes of death and change, until the end of all. And so the world goes on!

CHAPTER XII

REST

———

But go thou thy way till the end be: for thou shalt rest, and stand in thy lot at the end of the days.
—Dan. xii. 13.

THAT, of course, was a silent Sabbath, both in the manse and in the sanctuary, save only that the congregation that had assembled in ignorance of the event, joined together in solemn thanksgiving and prayer before they parted.

The four succeeding days were days of rest, marked only by the frequent visits of attached parishioners, who came to look once more on the precious dust, on which was stamped the calm majesty of death, together, too, with an almost youthful freshness, that carried us back to other years. Among these silent visitants, not the least deeply moved were the members of his Bible class, who had dwelt under his shadow to the last, and with that reverential fondness so beautiful in youth toward age, gathered up and cherished each gracious word of rich mellow wisdom that dropped from his lips.

On the Friday following (the 13th May), after an impressive service in the church, conducted by Drs. Henderson and Forbes of Glasgow, he was carried by devout men to his burial, amid a great concourse of concerned spectators, and followed by a numerous company of mourners, composed chiefly of relatives, parishioners, and the clergy of the district round.

He was laid to rest in the very spot where, to an assemblage not dissimilar, he had preached the glad tidings of the resurrection and the life twenty years before.

The funeral sermon was preached on the succeeding Sabbath, in a most appropriate and impressive manner, by the Rev. Dr. Smyth of Glasgow, one of his oldest and most valued friends, from the words, "Jesus Christ, the same yesterday, today, and for ever;" followed in the afternoon and evening by the Rev. Charles Stewart of Fort-William, son-in-law of the deceased, and the Rev. Alex. N. Somerville of Glasgow. Never was there a truer word spoken than that with which the last named preacher closed his affecting tribute to the departed, when calling upon his people "to take hold of the unstained mantle which their Elijah had thrown back from his ascending chariot," he appealed to them whether it were not a solemn thing to have had "such a minister of Christ going in and out among them day by day for nearly forty years, and yet not one of them had one word to say against him of reproach or of blame."

The following beautiful and touching tribute, kindly furnished by Dr. Smyth, from the conclusion of his sermon, I am tempted here to insert:—

"In 'calling to remembrance,' brethren, 'the former days,' you cannot fail, as a congregation, to cherish the most profound and affectionate reverence of the memory of your departed pastor. During a ministry extended considerably beyond the ordinary allotments of Providence, nearly forty years of which he laboured among you with all good fidelity in every department of pastoral duty, how weighty are the responsibilities under which you are placed for his invaluable services! Of those services it is hardly possible to form an exaggerated estimate. With talents of a decidedly superior order, literary and theological acquirements alike accurate and varied, depth and tenderness of spirit in addressing all classes of hearers, and pre-eminently distinguished by the Spirit of grace and of supplication—our beloved and lamented father was truly a master in Israel. 'In season and out of season,' when he had long passed the ordinary term of ministerial service, that aged disciple was ever found on the watchtowers of Zion. 'Jesus Christ, the same yesterday, and today, and for ever,' was the sum and substance of his preaching. He loved to dwell on the glory of his person, the perfection of his righteousness, the merit of his atoning sacrifice, and the prevalence of his intercession. 'His speech and his preaching was not with enticing words of man's wisdom, but in demonstration of the Spirit and of power.' Most faithfully, earnestly, and affectionately did he expound the doctrines, enforce the precepts, announce the terrors, and press home 'the exceeding great and precious promises' of the word of life. He shunned not to declare unto you all the counsel of God. 'As a scribe, instructed unto the kingdom of heaven,' your late revered pastor 'brought forth out of his treasure things new and old,' adapted alike to the conversion of the ungodly, and to the edification and comfort of the children of God. His theology was that of the good olden school of our Scottish forefathers, the Erskines, Fishers, and Bostons, of the last century, those men, 'mighty in the Scriptures,' whose names are identified with all that is sound in doctrine, and powerful in appeals to the conscience and the heart. His trumpet never gave an uncertain sound, but sent forth its voice 'not in words which man's wisdom teacheth, but which the Holy Ghost teacheth.' To how many in this congregation and neighbourhood, and in other places which occasionally enjoyed his ministrations, he was 'the savour of life unto life,' He only knows unto whom all things are naked and opened. 'The day will declare it.' Those seasons of spiritual revival with which this parish was signally blessed bore testimony to the seal which his divine Master was pleased to affix to his servant's fidelity; and may we not humbly hope that his removal hence may be still to some even as life from the dead? It is not of the public services only of your late honoured pastor that it is our privilege this day to speak. Following the footsteps of the apostle of the Gentiles, whose spirit he had largely imbibed, 'he taught you publicly, and from house to house,'—'warning every man, and teaching every man in all wisdom, that he might present every man perfect in Christ Jesus.' And were not those pastoral labours, whether in the family or among the lambs of the flock (for the young were very dear to his heart), or at the beds of the sick and the dying, or in the chambers of bereavement, and loneliness, and grief—all conducted in the spirit of Him who was meek and lowly in heart—who did not break the bruised reed nor quench the smoking flax—who spake 'a word in season' to satiate every weary, and to revive every sorrowful soul? Need I dwell on the bright example of Christian wisdom, consistency, and devotedness which shone forth in his daily life and conversation? 'Ye are witnesses, and God also, how holily, and justly, and unblameably he behaved himself among you that believe. As ye know how he exhorted, and comforted, and charged every one of you, as a father doth his children, that ye would walk worthy of God who hath called you unto his kingdom and glory.' ... We must not, dear friends, forget on the present occasion our departed father's leal-hearted devotedness to the Church of the Scottish Reformation—the Church of Knox, and Melville, and Henderson, and a noble band of men like-minded with them. The sacrifices which he so promptly and cheerfully made in vindication of the Scriptural rights and privileges of both pastors and people evince the value which he attached to the *exclusive supremacy* of the Lord Jesus Christ, as 'Lord over his own house;' 'the only Lord of the conscience' as well as of the Church and the nations. With inflexible decision, tempered and adorned with 'the meekness of wisdom,' did your beloved pastor uphold the purity of doctrine, discipline, and worship, whilst he cast in his lot with the Church of the Disruption, the Free Hereditary Protesting Church of Scotland. Its distinctive principles he held inviolably sacred; its enterprises of Christian philanthropy within our own borders and in the missionary field, whether among the 'dispersed of Israel' or 'far hence among the Gentiles,' occupied many of his thoughts, and called forth his prayerful and zealous co-operation. As a member of our ecclesiastical courts, we were often highly benefitted by his wisdom, and always gladdened and refreshed by his generous sympathy. We venerated whilst we loved him as a spiritual father, the father of our Presbytery, and latterly the father of our Church. Whilst the Church of which he was nearly sixty years a devoted minister was specially endeared to him, intertwined with his warmest affections and 'manner of life from his youth,' the Church in which surviving brothers and sons are still faithfully serving the Lord Christ—he rejoiced to hold cordial and confiding fellowship with the true Israel of God in all other sections of the Christian brotherhood. He was, in an emphatic sense, 'a lover of good men,' and delighted to 'keep the unity of the Spirit in the bond of peace' with all the disciples of the Lord Jesus—his Lord and theirs. We do not claim for the honoured dead exemption from those imperfections which are incident to all the saints of God so long as they are not completely delivered from 'the body of this death.' No man acknowledged more humbly and habitually that 'he had not already attained, neither was already perfect,' but no man 'pressed' more earnestly 'towards the mark for the prize of the high calling of God in Christ Jesus.' In simplicity and godly sincerity, not with fleshly wisdom, but by the grace of God, he had his conversation in the world. Having served his own generation by the will of God, he fell on sleep, and was laid unto his fathers. 'Mark the perfect man, and behold the upright, for the end of that man is peace.' 'Precious in the sight of the Lord is the death of his saints.' 'Here is the patience of the saints; here are they that keep the commandments of God and the faith of Jesus.' 'And I heard a voice from heaven, saying unto me, Write, Blessed are the dead which die in the Lord from henceforth, yea, saith the Spirit, that they may rest from their labours, and their works do follow them.'"

* * *

And so there passed away that calm, benignant spirit, around whom for some years past a kind of sacred halo had been gathering, as the venerable and almost the only surviving link between the present and the long past. He was, too, a peculiarly attractive representative of a type of the Christian pastorate which is, I suspect, rapidly becoming obsolete,—that of the quiet, steady, ongoing, conscientiously diligent and calmly earnest country minister, at once the father, the counsellor, and the friend of every man, woman, and child within his parochial bounds,—which is now giving place to the more impetuous and stirring, though in some respects also, perhaps, more one-sided energy of modern times. With the departure of the form may some portion, at least, of the old spirit still remain with us! If something of the listless languor of that old time has departed from us, may we not also have lost something of its repose. If in these times we have more holy activity, have we not also less of godly quietness,—if more haste, less momentum and less breadth? At least, it is worth considering whether that patient continuance in well-doing at all times, and in the worst times, for which our fathers were distinguished, might not be well combined with the more sanguine and aggressive zeal, in which many of us have got before them. Nor were the personal traits of our departed father less admirable, or worthy of reverential remembrance and imitation. At once a Nathanael and a John, he moved in an atmosphere of guileless sincerity and loving graciousness; though, at the same time, like the son of Zebedee, there was not wanting in him a latent element of sterner kind, which would now and then flash out, and turn the Barnabas into the Boanerges. If it was emphatically true of him that he was "a lover of good men," it was equally true that "he could not bear them that are evil;" nor were there many of his time more faithful in rebuking sin, or quick to mark by the clouded brow and pained, troubled look, the presence of aught that was unseemly or dishonouring to his Master. Yet even his anger was in great measure but another expression of love, being the indignant protest of the loving and generous heart against that which was unloving and "unlovely."[1] Often, too, the genial heartiness of the *way* would greatly mollify the sharpness of the *thing*, when he had occasion severely to chide. "O man!" he would say to the habitual dallier with strong drink whom he met casually by the way, "I would rather any day meet a cow on the road, with its honest face and sweet milky breath, than the like of you." The slight element of humour formed a kind of condiment to the bitter morsel, and made it go more sweetly down. But his habitual element was that of kind thoughts, kind words, and kind deeds. "There lies one," said a familiar friend of many years, while looking on the calm countenance and speaking lips from which the informing spirit had just

---

[1] A word often on his lips, as expressing that which was the only thing he might be said to hate.

fled,—"there lies one who never uttered a harsh word, or wanted a kind word to speak to high or low, rich or poor, among his people during all these long years." Something of this, no doubt, was due to a happy natural temperament, but much more to the chastening and hallowing grace of that Lord on whose bosom he leant, and beneath whose shadow he sat day by day. Thus in all respects following the steps of the "disciple of love," like him, also, he endured long,—lingering behind when brethren and companions of former days were, almost without exception, gone,—and falling asleep at length amid the veneration and love of a new generation and a new world.

In stature he was rather above the middle height, his figure stout and even portly, his countenance grave yet cheerful, and alike in youth and in age, "comely and well-favoured," while his gait, slow, measured, steady, whether in leisure walk or parochial round, seemed the very symbol and living embodiment of the quiet but steadfast tenor of his life.

Farewell, then, thou gentle and gracious friend of bygone days! May thy mantle fall and thy spirit rest in double measure on those that remain behind! "But go thou thy way until the end be; for thou shalt rest, and stand in thy lot in the end of the days."

ILLUSTRATIVE REMAINS

MODE OF CONDUCTING A REVIVAL:
ERRORS AND EVILS TO BE AVOIDED

Quench not the Spirit. Despise not prophesyings. Prove all things: hold fast that which is good.—1 Thess. v. 17.

THE branch of the great subject of the revival of religion allotted to me, is "The Mode of Conducting a Revival, so as to improve such a visitation of grace, with the description of the Errors and Evils to be guarded against." I feel my inadequacy to illustrate such a subject, and have endeavoured to approach to it in the spirit of humility, self-abasement, and prayer. There has, however, a previous question been moved, which may require, first of all, to be disposed of, namely,—"Is it right and lawful even to suggest or hint at such a thing as *conducting* a religious revival?

Is it not presumptuous? Is it not incongruous to speak of conducting a work which belongs exclusively to God, and in which the divine sovereignty is peculiarly prominent?" This has been in some degree already set on its true basis in discourses which have preceded in the course, particularly in that which illustrated the work of the Holy Spirit in the revival of religion, the sovereignty of God as connected with it, with the means of promoting the same glorious work.

I would now proceed more particularly to observe, in reference to the objection, that the figures which are employed by the great Teacher himself on the subject of which we are to treat, seem to furnish us with the proper answer to the question, and to the objections which have been started: "The wind bloweth where it listeth, thou hearest the sound, but canst not tell whence it cometh, or whither it goeth: so is every one that is born of the Spirit." Nevertheless human sagacity, industry, and activity, are much exercised and applied in making use of the winds in various branches of human enterprise, both on the land and on the water. And, although we cannot command the shower or the genial vegetative heat, the husbandman and the gardener know well how, with skill and activity, to prepare the soil and to cast in the seed: "This also, saith the prophet,[1] cometh from the Lord of hosts, who is wonderful in counsel, and excellent in working." The electrical fluid also has been, by later

[1] Isaiah xxviii. 29.

efforts of skill and ingenuity, directed in its course, so as to be conducted harmlessly along; and certain diseases to which the human frame is liable have been, by a well-known process of medical skill and experiment, either greatly modified or prevented, and all without any presumptuous attempt at interfering with the great all-wise Disposer,—the Lord of nature,—whose will gives law to the universe.

A revival of religion is an unusually successful dispensation of religious ordinances, the effect of a copious effusion of the influences of divine grace; but in other respects it comes under the same rules with the more ordinary dispensation, where the effects of the word of grace are less obvious and prominent. In both it is obvious that human agency is employed, and wisdom, and zeal, and activity are not less called for in the one than in the other, or rather a greater degree of prudence, of wise consultation, and of untiring watchfulness and activity, are to be called forth in the period of an awakening than in ordinary times. "In all our ways we are to acknowledge God, that he may direct our steps." The rules I have selected as the text are certainly peculiarly applicable in an awakened state of the Church: "Quench not the Spirit. Despise not prophesyings. Prove all things: hold fast that which is good," &c. Let us proceed, therefore, by the divine help and blessing,—humbly and earnestly implored,—first, to make some remarks upon the best mode of conducting and continuing a revival.

The first remark I would venture to make is, that "holiness to the Lord" should be inscribed upon *all* and everyone engaged in such a work. The Lord is in his holy temple, *therefore* should we keep silence before him. All who bear the vessels of the sanctuary should be holy. This, no doubt, is true at all times; but it holds still more pre-eminently and strikingly where the goings of the King of Zion are seen, with more than usual majesty and power, in his temple. "His arrows fly thick to pierce the hearts of the King's enemies, and the people fall under him." His word is "as a fire and a hammer that breaketh the rock in pieces." When all is thus, as it were, solemnizing—*the presence of Deity* peculiarly felt—the great work of the ever-blessed Trinity going on with unusual manifestation; when all heaven and hell, as well as earth, are, so to speak, in active and powerful movement; when the trumpet of the gospel waxes louder and louder; when even Zion Mount seems all on flame; and when an unusual influence attends the dispensation of the word, sealing it upon the souls both of sinners and of saints;— then the presence and the operations of the holders of office in the Church, who are characterized by anything but spirituality of mind, seems peculiarly incongruous.[1]

When religion is in a low state, it is seldom that the office of Eldership is at all filled up, even as to numbers, in any kind of proportion to the extent or population of parishes or congregations. There is, for the most part, a

[1] Deuteronomy xxiii. 9.

melancholy skeleton of what may have been at one time a well-conditioned, and fully organized, lively body of minister and of elders and deacons, in those parishes where religion has been in a declining state. But, even on the supposition that the framework has continued after the animating spirit of religion has departed, the dead branches must be replaced with those which have life from the true Vine,—the mouldering stones changed into living ones, ere the Church as a building, the temple of the Lord, can be restored to order or beauty. But perhaps in most cases where a "revival" takes place, one of the first movements is among *office-bearers* of the Church; and an improved state of that important department of Zion precedes any very decided or general improvement; in which case, these are "the Lord's remembrancers," ready to take their places on the watchtowers; and, making their rounds, "serving the Lord *instantly* day and night;" and, having grace and wisdom given to them according to their exigencies, they are in some degree prepared for the pleasant though difficult work to which they have been called. He "with whom is the residue of the Spirit" giveth more grace to the humble; and it shall be given, in the hour and season of need, how to speak, and to act, in answer to prayer,—secret and united.

This leads to another remark, that *prayer, unceasing* and *earnest*, is *that* wherein the great strength of a revival of religion lieth. This it is which draweth down the pure, life-giving, animating influence which sets all hearts in motion, which kindles every sacrifice, which consecrates every tongue, and makes every house a Bethel, every heart an altar and a sacrifice of a sweet-smelling savour, and each body and soul a living temple, consecrated to the presence and residence of the ever-blessed Trinity. Then every address to the Lord is the offering of the heart perfumed with the incense of the Redeemer's merits; every act of worship is an immediate, felt, realized entry into the holiest of all,—a beholding of the glory of God, and of Jesus Christ at his right hand,—a blessed communion "with the Father and with his Son Jesus Christ,"—"a pouring out of the heart before the Lord." There is a nearness to God felt and enjoyed, and a persuasion that "we *have* the petitions that we have desired of him." I know not anything by which the services of prayer and of preaching, which have been most evidently blessed for conversion and for edification, have been more peculiarly characterized and pre-eminently distinguished, than by this *prayerful, earnest* pleading with the Lord, that he may not leave to barrenness and coldness in the speaker, or to listlessness and unconcern in the hearers. It is not strength of arguing, or eloquence, in the ordinary sense of these expressions, which the Lord has owned and succeeded, but holy unction on the spirit,—humble, fervent wrestling, that the word may not return void, and that none may go away unimpressed; and this in secret, and *before* and *after* the addresses from the pulpit or prayer meeting. With regard to the social meetings for prayer, to which not a few have referred as the scene and the means of their first serious impressions, or where they found peace, the question has been put, How are they conducted, and what is their peculiarity, to which such more than usual success may be, under the blessing of God, attributed? The answer is in sum this: That they have not been so much for *increase* of knowledge and of experience in the Christian life, as for promoting lively personal religion, and to bring those to the *point* who have been, it may be, going *about it and about it*, without ever declaring "on the Lord's side." Fellowship meetings, properly so called, of Christian friends, for growth in grace and deeper insight into divine things, useful as they are, yet are *not* those which have among us been referred to; but those into which mere inquirers have been admitted, yea, which they have been solicited to attend. Some we know disapprove of this kind of prayer meetings as of a nature too open, and as wanting in correct views of Christian character, in allowing those to be present among the people of God who have not made any serious profession, and who may go away and bring discredit on the good cause. But perhaps this solution may be allowed, that prayer meetings of the nature now described, and fellowship meetings, are each in their place scriptural and useful; and, perhaps, that which might not be expedient in one grade of society may suit another. We have in our view chiefly those in the humbler walks of life, who are much more in the way of familiar and unceremonious converse with each other, and much less shackled by forms than those in a more elevated station. The meetings referred to are not so much for mutual religious fellowship, and the comparing of passages of Scripture or of experience, as for immediate addresses in prayer and praise, interspersed with a few verses of Scripture, comments and controversy excluded. Certain it is, that among us not a few *young parents* particularly have been thus much benefited; and either at such meetings, or as an effect of the reading and hearing of the gospel, and reflection and communings to which these meetings have given rise, not a few have been brought to the knowledge and experience of the truth.

The weekly public prayer meetings too, which have been conducted for several years, and to which some resorted who were not in the habit of church-going, have been blessed for conversion and for edification; to which we add, the meetings for missionary purposes, which have been found very enlivening,—so that, while "watering others, we are ourselves watered." No church or parish can be in a sound, wholesome, or flourishing state spiritually, where there is no special attention and prayer called forth in regard to the spiritual condition of the heathen and the Jew. Indeed, the very use of the prayer our Lord hath taught his disciples, condemns those who pay no respect to the spiritual wants and miseries of the Jewish or of the Gentile nations, and renders their use of such a prayer at any time a mere inanimate form. Too many parishes, we fear, are still in this sad and dead condition.

More closely still to the important point on hand, the concert of united, and continued, and persevering prayer for the abundant outpouring of the Holy Spirit, requires to be earnestly pressed and embraced. It has been remarked, as an important and encouraging fact in the history of the revivals with which we are best acquainted, that the moving spring of them all has been *prayer—believing, earnest, united*; by a smaller number, it may have been by only a very few at first, but, immediately preceding the remarkable awakenings, by a greater number of Christians brought together, as on sacramental occasions. Witness the wonderful day at the Kirk of Shotts in 1630, preceded by a night and a morning of incessant praying among ministers, and by the people who had been engaged in holy communion at the table of the Lord, and who were unwilling to depart without a blessing. Now, "the Lord's hand is not shortened that he cannot save, neither is his ear heavy that it cannot hear." When we come down to more recent awakenings in our Church,— to that of Moulin, 1800; Skye, 1814; Arran, 1813; Lewis, 1834; and in Kilsyth at this present time;—it is true in each case that "the Lord hearkened and heard those who feared his name," and who were "speaking often one to another" of the things of salvation, and who were, with united believing supplications, addressing the throne of grace, and were looking up and expecting an answer.

Going to Scripture history, and referring as far back as to the days of Enos, when "men began to call upon the name of Jehovah,"[1] and coming down to the day of Pentecost, when the apostles in an "upper room continued all with one accord in prayer and supplication, waiting for the promise of the Spirit," we find the same important place given to prayer; and, doubtless, the history of the true Church of the living God, in every age and in every place of the world, would be found to present a beautiful uniformity and unity in this respect, so that it is verified in the Church—the body of Christ collectively viewed, as well as in each individual member—that "whosoever calleth upon the name of the Lord shall be saved."[2]

I conclude this part of the subject, by earnestly pressing upon my fathers and brethren in the ministry, the duty and the privilege of having a weekly prayer meeting, wherever circumstances will allow of it, on some evening of the week, over which the minister should preside. The attendance, as it was formerly with us, for some time may be small and somewhat discouraging; but good is always doing *more* or *less*, and there may come a time when such a meeting will form a rallying-point to the inquirers after salvation, and a means of great comfort and edification to the people of God. Such weekly meeting was commenced in the year of the cholera, 1832, *with us*, as it had been in many places. It was often thinly attended,[3]

[1] Genesis iv. 26.
[2] Romans x. 12.
[3] That is, after that period.

but never given up. Not a few have obtained saving impressions when they dropped in to these meetings, where a familiar, short exposition of a Psalm was given with prayer and praise, and once in four weeks *religious* intelligence. It has been found by some to be to them the "house of God and the gate of heaven." Besides there were weekly meetings held in two rural districts, one of which has been recently formed into a parish, distinct so far as religious ordinances are concerned, which were found very conducive to spiritual good. In this latter case a *failure* was predicted, and seemed at one time *nearly verified*, but it was never given over to extinction; and now the work of the Lord has revived in that district, where, a few years ago, rudeness, ungodliness, and intemperance prevailed. We have just to reverse this description. Old things are in a great measure done away, and the Banton district of miners flourishes not merely by its minerals, but by prayer and the preaching of the word. A tap-room has been changed into a meeting-place for prayer, in which not a few assemble for holy converse and united prayer and praise, where lately there was only the sound of revelry and of wrangling! If it be asked wherein the great strength lies, the answer is, in *prayer*—without which the Church would be, like Samson without his hair, *weak and like others*.

Again, to carry forward and extend a revival while all the ordinary means of grace must be regularly and zealously maintained, there must be an instancy also *out of season.* Some have unreasonably objected to the using of any means beyond the usual Sabbath-day ministrations and the orderly round of visitation, as endangering due respect to the instituted regularly recurring means of grace; and such persons are so wedded to form, and so punctilious as to hours and seasons of public meetings, that the inroads made upon time and privacy of study by anything like an awakening of numbers to a sense of their spiritual danger, would be an annoyance to them. Now, my friends, while every studious and prayerful means should be used to conduct the preaching of the word, the devotional exercises in public, and the pastoral visitations, in the most pointed, lively, Scriptural, and edifying manner, giving to these the full force of all the preacher's head and heart, and best manner of address— there must be beyond these, and in addition to all the ordinary means, a *patient* and *instant* waiting upon cases of the convinced and anxious—that they may be instructed and edified; and even although the regular hours of closing should have arrived, the urgency of trembling and awakened inquirers *may*, yea, *must* in a season so unusual and an occasion so pressing, overrule all the customary, and at ordinary times, salutary restrictions as to times and seasons. I know this is with some a very difficult point, and, no doubt, it is easy to summon up reasons against all deviations from rule as to time and place for religious exercises. But the answer here is just this, that the whole work we are now treating of is of an unusual kind, and therefore must not be subjected rigidly to ordinary rules; here wisdom and zeal must be eminently conjoined with much and earnest waiting upon God for direction. The sunshine, while it lasts, should be fervidly improved, as it is by the farmer; the springtide must be waited on, and all hands must be at work—the sails spread, the prosperous gale with the favourable current not neglected, although the sun may have set, and although no moon nor stars should appear. The Philippian jailor was converted at midnight, and St. Paul once at least, when about to depart on the morrow, continued his speech until the same hour of midnight. So, my friends and brethren, even at *uncanonical hours* we must be willing that men be converted.

So it was with Mr. Robe in 1742, for "considering in his own mind what had been done at Cambuslang, and hearing the criticisms of the world on the week-day services—the many hours spent in church, &c., Mr. Robe, while he prayed for a time of refreshing from the Lord on his own people at Kilsyth, made various secret resolutions as to how he would arrange matters so as to avoid censure, should his prayers be answered. But when the time came, the exigence of the souls crying out, 'What shall we do?' overset all his preconceived plans; for when the good man had closed his services, and saw many of his people sit gazing upon him as if they were still hungering for more, he was constrained to begin anew, and then called in elders, and next ministers from the adjacency to assist, and also to mark the doings of the Lord," &c.[1]

Such seasons will *soon*, we fear *too soon*, pass by, leaving many after all in their dead sleep. The faithful, and rousing, and pointed preaching of the word, with appeals, it may be, *after* the usual addresses have been finished, without any apparent impression, may in some cases be called for, and have been actually attended with marked success, though here it is granted that there is room for the question, "Why resort to such methods, instead of leaving the message, solemnly and affection-ately delivered and followed with fervent effectual prayer, to the impression which may be expected to have been made?" In the method followed by our Lord and by the apostles, there seems to be warrant for both of these plans of addressing sinners. We find them in many instances declaring the truth boldly and affectionately, and this done, leaving it to operate by the divine Spirit's influence, just like the husbandman sowing the seed after previous preparation, and after a time looking for the increase. At other times we find them following up the more public and general addresses with special reasonings and conversations, so as "by all means to save some," even "pulling them out of the fire."[2]

One means which seems to have been often blessed to conversion, is that of individual address by one man,

[1] History of Revivals, &c., p. 260.
[2] Acts xxviii. 23, 30, 31.

or from one friend to another; as Andrew telling Peter, "I have found the Messias"—"Come and see." In the season of a revival this comes to be a very common case; the subject of salvation is so much the matter of interest and reasoning among friends and neighbours, that one member of a family speaks to another, and one workman speaks to his fellow, and one student in a class to another on the same bench, and one occupier of a seat in a church to the individual near him, in reference to the all-important subject. Thus it is that the reserve which is ordinarily observed on the subject of salvation is broken through, and there results a free and interesting interchange of thought, of mind, and of heart. Hence also arises very naturally an increasing number of meetings for prayer and Christian fellowship; and these again become so many rallying-points, or places of resort, to those who are asking the great question, "What they shall do to be saved." There is here, however, some evil to be apprehended when the anxious are led to go to the first person they meet with, however imperfectly qualified to give them advice. Surely it is to be regretted that it so frequently happens, that the sermon or the address which has made a serious impression is not immediately followed up by an earnest and humble application for advice to the teacher, whose words have been so far effectual; or, if that cannot be attained from any cause, why not to the godly parent, or elder, or stated pastor, or experienced Christian friend, instead of consulting only or chiefly with the most forward and self-confident, as is often the case; by which mistake many have been bewildered or led away to some new sect, and been turned aside to vain jangling? And here I would observe, that it should be well known and understood beyond all doubt, that consultation on soul-concerns is expected, and at all times welcomed and courted by the pastor watching for souls. This, alas! it must be acknowledged has been too seldom the state of things betwixt the minister and his flock; and thus many precious opportunities of doing good have been neglected, and many precious souls, there is reason to fear, have been lost.

Again, while prayer, as we have seen, is the *spirit* of a revival of religion, the substance of a revival,—the pillar and ground of all is the sound, zealous, pointed preaching of Christ,—the compliance with the command, "Go, stand, and speak unto the people all the words of this life." Some, it may be, have attempted to obtain or to promote a revival,—by speaking much about revivals, by describing them, or by *defending* them. All this may be so far well, and the recital at such meetings of well-authenticated cases of awakening and of conversion, may be very animating—yea, may be a *means of conversions*; but to rest in these,—to flatter ourselves that good has been done merely because a few meetings of this kind have been thronged by attentive hearers, will not do. The people must be plied from day to day with plain, faithful, Scriptural preaching *to* them, and not merely *before* them.

The conviction must more and more be wrought on the minds of the hearers, that the preacher is in earnest, that he means and feels what he says; that, in the words of R. Baxter, he "*never expects to meet any one of them in heaven unless they be truly converted.*" I have read of one preacher that he was successful in two things very difficult to attain,—the one is making the hearers to *feel* that *he* was in earnest in wishing their conversion; the other, that *God was in earnest* in calling them, and willing to save them. Of another I have heard, that lately he preached *about revivals*, but now he proclaims the doctrine of salvation more than before in a way calculated by the blessing of God really to *produce* a revival. It is the word of the living God, delivered in a living manner, which proves quickening and powerful! And here I would beg leave, with great humility, just to suggest the inquiry, whether the preaching of our day, generally speaking, has been altogether of the description for plainness, for godly sincerity, and home-dealing, which comes to men's business and bosoms; and, whether it would not appear, at the close of too many sermons, almost incongruous to expect that there may have been made such an impression as to lead any of the audience to stay behind, waiting and seeking further counsel? And further, may not the question be salutary, Are not some pulpit addresses, though unexceptionable as to doctrine, yet too much of an abstract description, and in the style of what is brought *before* an audience as hearers and judges, instead of being addressed *to them* as matters of personal and most pressing concern; and is not the sound too *general and uncertain* to leave a decided and deep impression? It is amazing, and it is lamentable, how many able and doctrinally sound discourses are delivered from Sabbath to Sabbath in the pulpits of our lands, of the practical, converting efficiency of which there are so few palpable fruits and evidences. Is there not too often a substitution of the *intellect* for the *heart*?—of human reasoning, for the demonstration of the Spirit? Is there not a defect of *prayer*, and a practical forgetting of the often-repeated text, "*Not by might, nor power*, but by my Spirit, saith the Lord of hosts?" Do we not *expect too little*, and *that* because we pray *too little*, and *too coldly*? Certain it is, that *there is* a *defect,—a great defect somewhere*, and we have probably touched upon some of the points in question, which may be useful in suggesting the remedy and the means of promoting a more awakened feeling and frame in speaking and hearing God's word. Of certain preachers who were peculiarly successful, it is said "their sermons are not distinguished by what is called *talent*; few of them exhibit marks of powerful genius: they are plain, energetic, and manly. No attempt at oratorical display; no poetical description; no metaphysical dissertation; no learned criticism; but *simple*, *practical* truth forcibly presented, illustrated, and applied." May the number of such preachers be increased a hundred-fold in all the Churches; may the Lord pour out his Spirit more copiously on preachers and hearers; then there will be a speaking as of dying men to dying men, *feeling themselves so*; and of *living men* to *living* men,—of *heart to heart!*

Another very valuable means of carrying forward the work of revival is *pastoral visitation*. Waiving all general remarks on the unquestionable importance of this department of ministerial duty, I would remark, that besides that these visits are from various causes generally few and far between, there is another imperfection too commonly attendant upon the mode in which they are conducted, and that is, too little holy earnestness and *closeness* and *familiarity* of the proper kind, similar to that of the inquiries of a beloved friend or family physician. There is apt to be too much ceremony, and too distant and too general and vague application, to be a likely means of leaving a permanent impression. Now, a season of revival affords manifest openings and facilities for closer and more home address. The awakening of so many to concern about salvation, and the beneficial change upon the life and conversation of neighbours and relatives, naturally give rise to a *more free*, and at the same time a peculiarly solemn mode of address. Such scenes bring into nearer contact with the condition of souls, and place us together as it were on the borders of eternity and the judgment-seat of Christ. We come at once to deal with our people,—young and old,—about matters of near and everlasting moment. Instead of a few remarks on relative duties, and it may be, hearing a few questions from the youthful members of the family, with a prayer—there will be (not forced in, but naturally introduced), serious conversation with each member as to how it now fares with them, and how their *souls* are? The idea I wish to convey is thus well expressed, in describing family visitation as practised by Presbyterian Churches transatlantic: "Visiting a family for the express purpose of religious inquiry, in order to ascertain the religious state of the heads of the family, and of every member; the amount of their Bible knowledge, and the manner in which they perform their acknowledged duties; and especially to ascertain whether they are really seeking God. The visit is purely pastoral; and as it is by no means considered requisite for the physician to travel all round the circle of general topics before he can venture to allude to the purposes of his visit, so neither is this deemed necessary for the minister; he feels at liberty at once to enter upon inquiries relating to the soul. These inquiries are often put in the plainest and most pointed form to the individual, and no evasion permitted. If the question be put, 'Are you living in the habit of prayer?' and the answer be evasive, it would be immediately followed by the plain question, 'Did you *pray this morning*? had you communion with God?' and followed by perhaps nothing more than an affectionate pressure of the hand, and a fatherly caution to beware of going back. Worldly conversation, perplexing inquiries, doctrinal disputes, find no place; the only subject is the application of the great doctrine of salvation to the consciences of the hearers, according to their capacities and attainments." Now, no doubt, wisdom is profitable to direct here, how far such close questioning may *in some cases* be practicable, or for edification; but certainly, holy zeal and affection may do very much to make *that* a very interesting work which is either too much neglected, or too formally and coldly performed, and make it a promising means of carrying forward a revival. A season like the present surely should be seized, for getting into more close dealing with the hearts and consciences of our people; and, in the majority of cases, having to deal with the poor and unlearned, access will be found more easily, and acceptably, and usefully than might at first be apprehended. Connected with this also, the catechetical and conversational manner of visiting families, in order to impart solid views of divine truth, and to establish the weak and lately awakened, is most requisite and desirable, seeing that it is through the influence of *family* religion that a revival of religion is likely to pervade and to be handed down in its blessed influence to succeeding times. (See the Directory for Visitation of Families, in our Confession of Faith.)[1]

[1] The following remarks appear to me very valuable: "From long observation of facts I have been particularly impressed with the importance of early instruction. I feel more strongly attached to the *good old way*, trodden by the venerable fathers of the Reformation in Scotland, and Holland, and England, and afterwards by our pilgrim fathers, who brought the light of 'immortality and light'

This brings me to speak of *Bible classes* for religious instruction conducted by ministers, and by pious and intelligent Christians under their superintendence. These have been greatly honoured of God as supplemental to the blessed and scripturally-approved example of "commanding children and household to keep the way of the Lord, and to do judgment and justice." There is warrant also for the Sabbath classes, for we read of one teaching his brother, saying, Know the Lord; and Cain's answer is recorded, *not* for approval, but as a *beacon*, "Am I my brother's keeper?" The answer is, "Yes, you *ought to care for a brother*; and especially for such as cannot, or will not care for themselves." True, every *family* should be a Sabbath school, and a prayer meeting—yea, a Church; but in order to bring about such a glorious result, every

---

to our western wilderness. With them the instruction of youth in the elementary doctrines of religion, by catechising and pastoral visitation, was an important part of ministerial labour. The revered *Flavel*, in 1688, addressing the Puritans, remarks thus: 'Prudence will direct us to lay a good foundation among our people by catechising and instructing them in the principles of Christianity, without which we labour in vain. Unless we have a *knowing* people, we are unlikely to have a *gracious* people. All our excellent sermons shall be dashed upon the rock of their ignorance. What age of the world has produced more lively and steadfast professors than the first ages? and then this duty (of catechising) most eminently flourished in the Church. Clemens, Optatus, Austin, Ambrose, Basil, were catechists.' This hath therefore been a constant practice in the Church; and in the first ages they had a particular person set apart to this office."— See Appendix to Sprague's Lectures (Collins's Edition), Letter X., by Dr. Proudfoot,—a most valuable letter, where all are excellent.

Scriptural means must be used, and such schools of the prophets as well-conducted Sabbath classes should be earnestly encouraged. On these the blessing of God has abundantly rested. Frequently has it been observed that, in revivals the Bible classes and Sunday schools have been deeply affected; *they* have felt the *first* influence of God's grace, and the great work has sometimes commenced with them. Before leaving this head, I would just observe, that from the *local plan* of Sabbath schooling, by drawing as it were a circle round a station, and collecting the neglected children enclosed, much good has resulted. Three years ago, by *thus* "*assaying to do good,*" a large call for Bibles resulted, and other blessed effects connected with the present revival—such as increase of prayer meetings, a desire for good reading, attendance on ordinances, *saving* benefit to not a few of youthful age.

Another means of carrying forward revivals is *the appointment of days of fasting and of thanksgiving.* I am persuaded that we are guilty of criminal neglect in this respect, in not being more observant of the spiritual and moral signs, as well as the occurring events which call for such appointments. The following, referring to the early history of our American Presbyterian brethren, seems to be well worthy of notice. Hutchison, in his history of Massachusetts, says, "The fathers laid aside the fasts and feasts of the Church of England, and appointed, as occasion required, days of fasting and prayer, to implore the divine blessing upon their affairs. This practice has been continued down to the present time (1829). If the savages threatened to exterminate their settlement, the fathers appointed a *fast*; if religion languished, they held a *solemn fast*. At different periods this practice has been observed ever since among the Churches; and very frequently have great blessings been granted, after days of supplication, accompanied by solemn fasts. So of days of thanksgiving." Upon this subject I would very humbly suggest that congregational or parochial *fasts* and *thanksgivings*, occasioned by some more than usual breaking forth of *evil* on the one hand, or of *good* on the other, seem highly beneficial. The experiment was made in the parish of Kilsyth, in the year 1830, on account of appalling moral depravity prevailing. The appointment was much honoured of God and respected by man, though at first opposed by some. The reasons for it were set forth in a memorial by the session, and read for two Sabbaths previously. It was followed by a blessing. All the Commandments were gone over, in a portion of the sermon as well as in *prayer*, and special, very special, notice of the *breaches* that had been most prominent. That day is still remembered by many, and referred to with interest. *The first day of this year* (1840) *was a thanksgiving day and a prayer day*. A similar appointment was very lately made by one of the brethren in Edinburgh, owing to the inadvertent admission of some unworthy communicants, the observance of which had a very solemnizing effect, and, I believe, has not been without its visible good fruits. This is a course which ought to be more frequently resorted to. Before an ordination, for example, how suitable to have a day, or a part of it, spent in fasting and prayer. In the first platform of Presbytery after the Reformation, as described in the Geneva Confession, this is to be found.[1]

But these observations, though referring to points of great importance, under the head of means of carrying forward revivals, may be perhaps judged too general, and more specialty may be demanded. These specialties, however, may more properly be dealt with under the second head.

II. *Errors to be guarded against* in the matter of revivals.

Errors and mistakes indeed are incident to everything to which man puts his hand. In the case of ordinary duties, the danger is formality. In services and duties more unusual, as in the case of the work of revival, the errors to which ministers and office-bearers are exposed are of a different character; either, on the one hand, in being too easily satisfied with cases, in healing too slightly, and being too ready to give comfort; or, on the other, in putting stumbling-blocks in the way, and

---

[1] "The ministers and elders, at such times as there wanteth a minister, assemble the whole congregation," &c. "At the which time the minister exhorteth them to humble themselves to God by fasting and prayer (Acts xiii. 14, &c.), that both their election may be agreeable to his will, and also profitable to the Church."—"Geneva Confession," received and approved by the Church of Scotland, 1560, John Knox being minister.

denying the application of the balm of consolation where it ought to be administered. Certain it is, on the one side, that awakening, conviction, weeping and trembling, are *not conversion*, though often the commencement of a saving change; therefore there should be a sifting process as a preliminary to comforting. On the other hand, it is the divine will and command that each one to whom the gospel offer is made should immediately believe, and so have life, without being kept for weeks, or even days, in despair; and, therefore, we are sure that there is no Scripture warrant for keeping anxious inquirers a certain length of time in legal bondage and labouring in the fire ere the free offer of salvation is made to them. Again, there is an error into which those not acquainted with the work are very apt to fall, and that is, when there appears to be any melting and evident commotion among the hearers, straightway to get alarmed, and to wish to have all the subjects of such distress instantly removed; and again, to become impatient of detention—to wish, in short, to shut all up decently, it may be with a few words of prayer and advice, and so to conclude. There is a great and manifest danger of thus quashing and deadening convictions both in the distressed and in attendant friends and observers. In relation to the question, *what is duty* when—as is sometimes, though not always the case in such awakenings—there are sobbings or outcries of the spiritually-wounded, I will here recite some of Mr. Robe's observations on this subject, with this remark that, when we were tried exactly in a similar way recently, in the church-yard scene which I have elsewhere described, we followed the same plan as Mr. Robe had been led to pursue, without any special reference at the time to his mode and the reasons he assigned. Similarity of cases led to a similar treatment. Mr. Robe had been previously anxious on this subject, and had made resolves that so soon as any fell under remarkable distress, they should be carried out of the congregation into a separate place; he also prayed that, if it were the holy will of God, he would bring them to a sight of their sin and danger without those bodily distresses, which were so unpleasant to behold, so distressing to the people themselves, and offensive to several. "The Lord in a little time discovered to me my error and imprudence in this. … I observed that some were awakened while they had the distressed in their sight, and heard exhortations given in the place where they were convened. From this I was persuaded that the example of others under spiritual terrors and distress was one of the means the Lord was pleased to bless. … I am now of opinion, after all I have seen and experienced relative to this work, that it is best to leave the distressed to their liberty, and in the congregation, if they incline, until it be dismissed. No means that Providence puts into our hands is to be omitted that hath a tendency to awaken secure sinners."

In these sentiments I entirely accord with my venerated predecessor. In reference to one of the remarkable days of the present revival already noticed, I may just farther remark that I felt a tendency to the error Mr. Robe says he fell into at the first—namely, to take away the distressed by themselves, which would have left many equally anxious unaddressed, and might have arrested the progress of the work, and prevented much of the good which we know resulted from continued appeals; for we know that the Lord works by the use of means, and that sympathy with and reasonings *from the case* of the distressed are among the means which he is pleased to employ. The few sentences following are from the remarkably judicious letter on this subject addressed to Mr. Robe, and introduced into his narrative: "If the King of glory descends in his majesty among you, and strikes secure sinners with the terrors of his wrath, whereby they are made, from a felt sense of their perishing condition, to cry out, 'What must I do to be saved?' why must these trophies of his victory be removed out of the assembly? This cry is what was common in the apostles' time, and no doubt will be so again, and much more abundant as the glory of the latter day approaches." And again— "Christ will plead his own cause, and wisdom is justified of her children." How true also is that which follows, of which I have often thought since the beginning of this work: "There is no end, and there can be no good fruit of seeking to obviate the objections of an ungodly world, and the company of carnal, worldly professors. Their cavils will be innumerable," &c. In reality one of the greatest errors to be dreaded, and watched, and prayed against, is that of excessive caution under the guise of prudence, in anxiety to avoid giving offence to worldly people, who can never be reconciled by all you can do, to anything in the shape of a revival of religion. We never should attempt to make it palatable to those who cannot suffer anything like vital religion in any form. No doubt the good moral effects resulting the men of the world may be competent in some degree to appreciate, and it is good to have these to appeal to in answering objections; but in the conducting of the revival itself, there must be no respect to what worldly friends may say, or even to the opinion of cold-hearted professors, who are too easily satisfied to let things go on as they are, rather than take much trouble or run any risk of being excepted at by the friends of what has been called *rational religion*. Needless offence is not to be given, nor are we to be regardless of the censure of observers further than a sense of duty and the command, "Be not conformed to the world," demand; but we apprehend, after all, that the error of excessive caution is much more common among us[1] than

[1] I have said, "*among us*," for it appears from various passages in the valuable appendix to Sprague's Lectures, that in America there are lamentable excesses and follies connected with the subject of revivals. I quote the following sentences from an able and judicious letter of Dr. Griffin, as a warning against all that would justly prejudice the cause: "Let the attention of the world be aroused by every hallowed means; let the imagination and passions be wrought upon as far as the most sweet, and solemn, and awful truths of God can move them; let every knee be pressed to the earth in prayer, and

the opposite of too much zeal, while, most certainly, all things should be "done decently and in order." This is a general salutary rule, for God is the God of order in all the Churches. Nevertheless the Lord worketh variously, and sometimes as it were cometh out of his place, making bare his arm, and there is a flying thick of his arrows, piercing many hearts, and breaking of rocks with a kind of loud explosion. Sometimes, again, it may be truly said that there "cometh the sound of earthquake, and of strong wind;" and yet the Lord is not in these, "but in the still, small voice," calling to solemn reflection and deep musing. In all meetings of God's people, let us ever remember that we stand in awe: "The Lord is in his holy temple, let all keep silence before him."

Another evil to be guarded against in a season of revival is, the intrusion of *controversy* and of *novel doctrines*; not new, it may be, in actual existence, but as relates to the place and the people where the awakening may be in progress. "Beware," says the judicious Halyburton, "beware of vain speculations and curiosities in religion." These tend sadly to blight the springing of the ear of grace, if, indeed, they do not choke it even in

---

every authorized tongue be strained with entreaties to dying men; let the whole operation be as impressive, as irresistible, as love, and truth, and eloquence can make it. But oh, for the honour of Christ and his Spirit, and in pity to the cultivated millions of our race, let revivals be conducted with order and taste (and, we add, with Scriptural simplicity and unction), and shun everything by which our brethren may be offended or made to fall!"

the blade. This applies to societies and classes as well as to individuals. In Glenlyon the introduction of the controversy about infant baptism proved most injurious to the revival which had begun, and which, previously to this unhappy controversy, was advancing so auspiciously. The enemy got advantage, and instead of the all-important questions, "What shall I do to be saved?" and "How are we to grow in grace?"the torch was thrown in, and the community set in a flame about the mode and the subjects of baptism. The former of these—the question about dipping and immersion, is usually introduced in the first place (though assuredly of minor importance), which, when practically illustrated by the actual immersion of a few, gives to the careless, to scoffers, and to formalists, just what they wish, in order to involve the whole matter of religious revival in ridicule, and to turn men's minds away entirely from the real controversy which is carrying on against the stupidity, worldliness, and irreligion of an untoward generation, and for the destruction of "all the works of the devil." The attempt has been repeatedly made in Kilsyth by certain of the American Baptists, who, by the way, are very unsound in their creed in essential points: while the *particular Baptists* have not been amenable to the censure of bringing forward their peculiar views, but, as far as known to us, have rejoiced in the work of grace, and wished us success. We have much reason to be thankful that the class I have referred to above have been hitherto defeated entirely, and that their attempts to distract prayer meetings by introducing their favourite subjects have been most strenuously and *harmoniously* resisted. The attempts of the Roman Catholics, and of Socinians, and the teachers of universal pardon, have been equally unsuccessful. I am happy to say that our people cannot endure *unsound* doctrine; and when they hear the word as they have heard it from a great number of ministers from various places of the Church, they have shown the opposite of a captious spirit, and have, we know, been much delighted and edified with the uniformity of Scriptural doctrine, with which they have been so highly favoured. "The sheep of Christ hear his voice, and a stranger will they not follow." Yet we are justly jealous of such strangers making entry, and of "grievous wolves not sparing the flock."

When I speak of the danger of controversy to the on-going of a revival, I wish not to be misunderstood, as if the true faith in its whole extent were not to be uniformly maintained, and as if a genuine revival were not in fact just a powerful and successful combat with error in doctrine and in practice. Instead of hanging out a flag *of truce* to the Arminians, for example, the great truths which are so fully set forth in the epistle to the Romans have been illustrated and expounded, as an antidote to their errors during two years past. It was not then by avoiding controverted subjects, and simply dwelling on truths common to professing Christians, as some would recommend, but by "not shunning to declare the whole counsel of God;" by dwelling on every doctrine of the Bible, whether controverted or not, or however repulsive to the carnal mind, and by bringing all to the test of Scripture, that the work was promoted. What, in fact, has a Christian to do but to carry on a constant, unremitting warfare with error, both doctrinal and practical—a casting out and killing bad seed, and sowing and watering the good?

I cannot refrain here from just hinting, in relation to a very stirring subject at present, that nothing could be conceived more threatening to the ongoing of such a blessed work as that we are privileged to witness, than would be the INTRUSION of a *minister* in opposition to the seriously felt and solemnly expressed convictions of the people that they could not be spiritually edified by his ministrations. If the calling for the serious, prayerful consideration of this subject at the present crisis of our Church, should be viewed by any one as an infringement of the rule I have been illustrating,—namely, the evil influence of controversy, I would only say in addition to what I have just advanced, that in our apprehension, we might as well at once abandon the Church of our fathers, dear as it is to us, in which, in 1742 and in 1839, such glorious things have been done for us, whereof we are glad, as continue in stupid inactivity, when the enemies of her true interests would deal with her as the Philistines with Samson, when, his strength having departed, they proceeded to put out his eyes, and make him grind in the prison-house, the sport of his enemies. Surely we should be already blind and enchained, did we not arise as one man to use all diligence that our views and wishes on this subject may not be mistaken. Surely our thus praying unceasingly for the prosperity of our Sion, and our holding fast that which is good, and our not *despising prophesying*, as those do who put nothing to the account of interesting, and unctuous, and sound preaching of the word (which are very essential elements of acceptable ministrations), but who think anything which is not absolutely heathenish and heretical good enough for our people,—our taking a strong view of the present position of our Church, as calling for all our earnestness of prayer and exertion, cannot be amenable to the charge of "quenching the Spirit," whose office it is to *testify* of Jesus Christ, as the Church's Head and great Shepherd. In this great cause it is good to be zealous, and we use weapons, *not carnal*, "but mighty through God to the pulling down of strongholds."

Further, to *promote*, *consolidate*, and *perpetuate* a revival, let us be on our guard against superficial and ill-cemented systems of religious doctrine and practice. In a period of awakening, the feelings are excited, the conscience roused; exercises of prayer and praise much engaged in; *psalmody* is unusually lively; the *hymn-book* is by some converts specially exercised; but the *Catechism* and the Confession of Faith, and even the Sacred Scriptures themselves, are in danger of being in a measure neglected. In a sound revival, certainly the word of the living God, the grand means of regeneration, and of progressive holiness, must be prized above all other books; and so we are happy to find it generally among us: yet some of the awakened have been, it is frankly acknowledged, but very imperfectly grounded in the principles "of the faith delivered to the saints." Some of them never had the form of sound words at all; by others all had been forgotten in the days of their ungodliness. If, therefore, pains be not taken to communicate solid, Scriptural views, and to indoctrinate both the head and the heart, there may be anticipated a plentiful crop of very green weak stalks, which may never ripen at all, or which will produce at best only a very small quantity of good grain. There is much need therefore to be at all due pains, both in preaching publicly, and in teaching privately from house to house, to explain clearly and fully, and, at the same time, *affectionately* and *attractively*, the doctrines and the duties of Christianity, and the close connection betwixt them; so that the word of Christ may *dwell* in the converts *richly*, and that they may learn to do all, in word and in deed, in the name of the Lord Jesus Christ; giving thanks through him; and teaching and admonishing themselves and others; "building up in their most holy faith, praying in the Holy Ghost, keeping themselves in the love of God, and looking for the mercy of the Lord Jesus Christ unto eternal life." There must be much watchfulness, lest when men sleep the enemy sow tares, which will grow up much more readily and luxuriantly where there is a lack of good seed sown.

Another error I would point at is, the yielding to the opposing influence, and the failing of ardour to push the advantage gained, and being in a manner satisfied that enough has been gained, or at least as much as can be expected; the conviction that we need not look for the continuance beyond a certain limited period of such a lively state of religion in a parish or congregation; in short, a taking it almost as a matter of course, that after a *revival* there shall be a *decline*. This, indeed, is what the enemies of such a work are always setting forth, as an objection to any work of this kind, that any benefit which might seem to be gained by the awakened energies and feelings of Christians in such a season, is more than counterbalanced by a consequent depression, or even an outbreaking of opposite passions and feelings. Now, there is certainly *no necessity* for such an unhappy result; no reason why the increase of the power of religious truth over the mind, and conscience, and hearts of men should be attended with so deplorable a result as that which has been alleged. On the contrary, as is true of evil, that a "little leaven leaveneth the whole lump," so also is it true of good. True religion is both of a diffusive and of a perpetuating quality. Genuine piety is not like the seeds which are called annuals; it is rather of the perennial kind. Still, the objection of the enemies of revivals, that they are apt to prove like the morning cloud and early dew, may, and ought to be improved upon, as showing us what we should guard against, and that with much concern, with continued care and diligent use of the means, especially with earnest prayer. Let not diligence be relaxed, nor prayer cease, nor concert for united intercession and pleading be broken or intermitted. Mr. Robe laments this in 1749, and says, "Had the concert been renewed which had begun about 1744, who can tell but that the revival would have been much more extensive and continuous? The means already pointed out may, by the divine blessing, secure this most desirable result. But among the errors to be watched and guarded against, this of losing heart, and lowering or stinting our expectation, or shortening our aim, is to be particularly noted; and in opposition to this error, as the Apostle Paul exhorts,[1] "Let us labour,"—the word signifies let us be *ambitious*,— "that whether present or absent, we may be accepted of him." Let us not only "hold fast that which we have, that no man take our crown," but seek with intense holy ardour of sacred ambition, that the temple of the Lord may be carried on, and raised still to a more elevated and commanding height, pointing to the skies. Let not the builders slacken their exertions; let not the watchers go to slumber. Let the Lord's remembrancers not keep silence, but "give him no rest till he establish and make Jerusalem a praise in the earth."

[1] 2 Corinthians v. 9.

I will advert to another error, which we may be in danger of falling into in a season of revival; or rather, an error on the right and left,—namely, the error on the one hand of a reluctance to go to any extent beyond the regular dispensation of religious ordinances; and the opposite error of making more of the extraordinary, to the disparagement of the regular and weekly dispensation of word and sacrament. The preaching of the word not only out of the usual seasons, but also out of the *usual place*, some people have such an aversion to, that the very fact of sermons delivered to crowds in a market-place, or church-yard, and the congregating such numbers of people at the communion, are regarded by them with suspicion, if not positively condemned; but the facts are unquestionable, that by this going out as it were to the highways and hedges, many poor wanderers have been brought in; and the influence of the truth much more extensively diffused than could have been otherwise; the seed of the word has in this way been carried far beyond the boundaries of a small district, and not a few added to the Church of such as shall be saved. The dispensation of the supper in the unusual circumstances of a parish where there is a revival, seems to possess the advantage, besides its direct end in the edification and comfort of newly-converted disciples, of causing the word of the gospel to come to the ears and hearts of many who might not otherwise ever know the joyful sound, and of quickening the affections and graces of God's people.

The assembling, too, in the house of God much more frequently than in ordinary times, while the desire for hearing continues, and sowing in large measure the good seed, assuredly is the part of wisdom, and accordant with the maxim and practice of the wise preacher, who "still taught the people knowledge;" and the rule, "In the morning sow thy seed, and in the evening withhold not, for thou knowest not which shall prosper—*this* or *that*, or whether both shall not be alike good." Beware, then, of the error of withholding abundance of good seed, and of neglecting to afford opportunities of hearing the word; for if you do, the enemy will be at work, and sow a plentiful crop of weeds, which will grow up luxuriantly. To prevent chaff, and worse, even bad seed getting in, fill up the vessel and then the ground with abundance of good seed—even sound and healthful doctrine.

On the other hand, it would be an error still worse than the former, were we to give any kind of prominence to the extraordinary, above the ordinary and regularly recurring means of grace, to prefer the prayer meeting to the church, or to give any countenance to the idea, that there is some unaccountable virtue or charm in an *out-of-door* sermon, or in the congregating of multitudes, which in vain may be looked for within a church or in the ordinary Sabbath-day worship. Our Lord assures us, that "wherever two or three are gathered together in my name, there I am in the midst of my people. Lo! I am with you *always*."

I have remarked an evil which did incidentally and in part result from ministers about forty years ago so often leaving their own churches vacant, that they might assist at communions, the consequence of which was that too many of the people relaxed their attendance on the weekly returning Sabbaths, feeling no reluctance, nor thinking it any breach of the Fourth Commandment, to remain in their houses every now and then, as the appearance of a shower of rain, or of snow, or even as indolence suggested. Now, it is worthy of consideration, that the frequently repeated meetings for worship during a period of revival, unless there be much pains and prayer directed to meet and obviate this evil, may lead or rather be perverted to this very hurtful end, namely, a sinful neglect of gathering the manna fresh every day and every Sabbath. There is certainly this evil to be anxiously guarded against, a depending on new excitements, instead of hearing what "the Spirit is daily saying to the Churches." The regular exercises of worship and ordinary means of grace may be compared to the regular channels and conduits through which the waters are conveyed, which keep them from overspreading and demolishing the surface exposed to them; and these being kept always open and in repair, the unusually copious descending of vapour in the abundant showers, or even the flood, has conductors prepared, and in a state of readiness to receive it. In fine, the great and *summing* evil, if we may so express it, is just the "*quenching* the Spirit." We know what quenches flame, to which there is an allusion in the text. It may be quenched by being overlaid; so is the Spirit by the cares of the world, by cold speculation. Fire is quenched by *neglect*, by being left unstirred; so is the Spirit by not stirring up the gift; or by withholding material; so, in a spiritual sense, by not supplying the fuel of meditation and reading the word and prayer; or by *want* of air, or by foul air; for flame goes out in an exhausted receiver, and is extinguished by pouring impure air upon it, or water, or any other element adverse to it; so is the Spirit quenched by the exclusion of the holy atmosphere of heavenly desire, and by unsavoury temper and conversation, or by conformity to the world and secularity of spirit, especially in ministers and elders. The livid flame of envy and malice, too, eats out the holy fire of divine love; and, as the separation of the embers, and scattering and dividing the material which feeds the flame, soon cause the fire to go out; so the divisions among brethren quench the Spirit, and arrest the progress of *revival*.

Here I would further suggest, in concluding this head, that there is need of much grace to establish and keep the heart, for Satan is always busy, and when shut out at one avenue he will try another. When he cannot get us inveigled in the snares which have been detected and broken, he will try to get us to worship some other idol, and to make even duties a snare; he will come even into *prayer meetings* when other meetings are abandoned; and he will try to pervert these by spiritual pride—by speculation—by setting some of the members, whose natural temper may have that tendency to vie with others which shall pray most fluently; and may be tempting us to speak of the *number* of our prayer meetings, as if these were the certain and almost the *only* evidences required of real godliness and of growth in grace. Thus we fear the Spirit of God has often been grieved away; and even prayer meetings may have become the germs of division instead of godly edifying. We cannot be too much on our guard in these respects, for grace is a plant of a tender kind, and so is a *revival* of a *tender* and delicate nature. Let none of these social prayer meetings be a substitute for the domestic altar, or the secret worship of the closet. Let us "keep the heart with all diligence, for out of it are the issues of life." Let there be a Church in every house—and let every heart be an altar. Thus, instead of quenching the Spirit, we must earnestly invite his stay; we must hate and renounce those sins which cause this "holy dove to mourn, and which would drive him from our breast." In our own spirits—in our families—in our Church—there must no wicked thing be endured. Strict *discipline* among our reputed converts, and in our members generally, must be exercised; a fast day may very soon be required, and we humbled because of the sins which we fear may be committed in the management of this matter, which will be peculiarly aggravated after what has been *seen, and tasted, and professed*. Here we may truly apply our Lord's words on a certain occasion, in answer to the question of a disciple, "Why could not we cast him out?"—"this kind goeth not out but by prayer and fasting."[1] It is not by mere "bustling activity," nor by wisely-laid and strenuously prosecuted schemes of either Church reform or enlargement; it is not by good planning, nor good writing and reasoning, nor by large donations, nor by earnestness of zeal—no, not by all these combined that the blessing is to be secured. All these are good and needful, but they require to be all consecrated by prayer—drawing down the unction of the Holy Ghost. While, therefore, we plan, and labour, and plant, let us also water; for "God, the hearer of prayer, giveth the increase;" "as for God, his work is perfect;" with him is the residue of the Spirit. He promises to send, not only the soft dew unto Israel, but "water upon the thirsty, and floods upon the dry ground."

I have thus attempted the part assigned to me in this course on the interesting work of revival, treating of the "mode of conducting it, and pointing out errors to be avoided." I fear that what R. Baxter remarks will be but too applicable here, that upon everything that "man touches, he leaves the marks of his fingers." Yet the Lord, whose work every genuine revival is, *can*, and *will*, notwithstanding, maintain and carry forward his cause, as again his voice is distinctly heard in his Church, crying, "Prepare ye the way of the Lord; make straight a high way; let every valley be exalted, and every mountain

---

[1] Matthew xvii. 21.

levelled; and the crooked and rough places made plain, that Jehovah alone may be exalted." Verily, "revival" has come most seasonably. No time, it is true, is *unseasonable*; but in many points the present is a very perilous and momentous crisis; and nothing, we are persuaded, could save us but a *powerful* awakening from the deadly slumbers of spiritual insensibility, and the pervading influence of genuine godliness. There is only one way to regenerate society—the same by which the individual is regenerated; namely, "by the word of truth, which liveth and abideth for ever." The first teachers of Christianity had no devices, but those of plain truth and strong faith, and humble boldness, and fervent love; and the giving themselves to prayer and the preaching of the word. Let it be said of us, as of them, "We believe, and therefore speak; we feel, and therefore persuade; we desire to do nothing *against*, but *for*, the truth, that God in all things may be glorified, through Jesus Christ; to whom be glory now and for ever!"

SERMON I

PREACHED IN THE CHURCH-YARD[1] OF KILSYTH, AUGUST 12, 1838

Thy dead men shall live, together with my dead body shall they arise. Awake and sing, ye that dwell in dust: for thy dew is as the dew of herbs, and the earth shall cast out the dead.—ISA. xxvi. 19.

YOU were previously aware, my friends, from what text we intended to address you this evening—the words which I have now read in your hearing. They were inscribed in Hebrew characters on the tombstone of his wife by the Rev. J. Robe.[2] Near

---

[1] It was at these church-yard services that the old domestic pulpit mentioned in Chapter I was finally called into requisition. It, however, at last gave way under the severe strain of the impassioned preaching of those stirring days.

[2] The fact that the words of the text were engraved by Mr. Robe

that stone he himself rests, and his ministerial zeal and eminent success, specially during the years 1742-1743, in the conversion of souls, have erected for him a monument more lasting than any reared by human hands, and formed of the most costly and durable material. Eighty-four years have run on since his mortal remains were

---

on the tomb-stone of his wife in *Hebrew* characters is suggestive. It reminds us that he and others of his time, who were instrumental in the revival of God's work, were not mere religious enthusiasts (as the world would call them), that they were men of erudition as well as ministers of Christ. It is well known that the famous Thomas Boston of Ettrick was profoundly versed in the Hebrew language; and it may be mentioned that the pious and learned Dr. Gillies of Glasgow persevered in the study and published a manual of the language. Dr. Maculloch of Cambuslang also attained to some proficiency in the same department of scholarship. And such reminiscences naturally recall the honoured names of James and Andrew Melville, and the appearance of the latter with his Hebrew Bible in his girdle before King James. "There were giants in those days." In later and darker times—the times of dead moderatism—the study of the language declined, and anything like an accurate knowledge of it was not to be found; indeed, it came to be a common proverb among students, "Hebrew roots in a barren soil." The students were generally satisfied with such a knowledge of Latin and Greek, and perhaps of one of the modern languages, as was sufficient to gain for them admittance into a family; anything beyond this they did not think of seeking to acquire. In these later years we are glad to notice that interest in the oldest of the sacred languages has revived, and that an eminent degree of proficiency in it is by no means uncommon, and we trust that while God's "work and power appear" again as in the days of old, there will continue to be a learned as well as a holy and earnest ministry.—*Note by Author, added April* 1859.—As to Hebrew studies, see his own practice, Chapter III. of this Memoir.

laid in the dust close to the spot on which I now stand. The usual emblems of mortality and of the swift and imperceptible lapse of time are rudely sculptured on the stone—the ship before the wind, the hour-glass, the quickly moving shuttle, together with symbols of the mortal, putting on immortality, and of the trumpet summoning to judgment.

But the words of the text inscribed on the open volume express more plainly than any emblem or hiero-glyphic the triumphant hope of the blessed who die in the Lord. The letters are *there* in a language to most of us here unknown, and they have been almost obliterated by the wasting of the elements; but, blessed be God, they are *here quite legible*, as you can all read them in the Bibles in your hands, in your own tongue. What cause have we for gratitude, my dear friends, that it is so; that we have not to decipher the characters before us; that the grand and blessed doctrine is not sealed up in a language known only to the learned, or written in characters which time and the elements can obliterate, but conveyed to us in language familiar, and which cannot be misunderstood, "life and immortality being brought to light by the gospel." Job, in ancient days (even as early as the days of Abraham) expressed his belief in the doctrine of the text. He wished his words to be written in a book, to be engraven upon the rock, and lo! it is fulfilled; they are in the faithful record, and more clearly and fully known than if they had been literally committed to the memorial of solid rock, even the most impervious to the waste of time. Hear the profession of his faith and of his hope in a resurrection to life: "I know that my Redeemer liveth, and that though after my skin worms destroy this body, yet in my flesh shall I see God, whom I shall see for myself, and not another; though my reins be consumed within me" (Job xix. 25-27).

As it is intended to set up a monument in memory of the good and eminently honoured minister to whom we have already referred, whose name is so closely associated with the interesting revival of religion in 1742, and as we wish now to improve the occasion, we have chosen the text which he inscribed on the tombstone of his first wife as the subject of this discourse. May the Lord vouchsafe his presence, favour, and special blessing!

Let us endeavour, then, to improve the subject and occasion by explaining, in the first place, the text and context; by presenting, secondly, some views of the chief doctrine which is set forth in it, and for which it has been selected as appropriate; and by noticing, thirdly, some of the instructions we are to derive from it.

I. In reference to the text and context, I would observe that as in the *thirty-seventh chapter of Ezekiel*, where the resurrection of the dry bones in the valley of vision is described, the primary reference is to the restoration of Israel—to their recovery "as life from the dead," an event yet future, but certain, and probably now near its accomplishment. Many have been the alternate depressions and elevations of God's people, but we are assured that they shall yet be exalted. "In that day will I make Jerusalem a burdensome stone for all people: all that burden themselves with it shall be cut in pieces, though all the people of the earth be gathered together against it." The "other lords" who had had dominion over God's people are represented as "dead, they shall not live, they are deceased, they shall not rise, their memory shall perish." Contrasted with this degradation and punishment to which the enemies of the people of God were doomed is the blessed promise of the text: "Thy dead shall live." Those that seemed to be dead, who had received sentence of death in themselves, who were cast out as if naturally dead—they shall appear again in the native vigour of life. The Spirit of life shall come from God, shall enter the slain, and shall raise up the dry bones as a mighty army of living men. However low they may be brought, they shall arise—even Jerusalem, though now lying as a dead body or carcase to which the eagles are gathered together. And, therefore, let the poor and scattered remains of God's ancient people now dwelling in the dust awake and sing, for they shall yet see Jerusalem in the glory of its former life. The dews descend upon the herbs which have been parched all day by the sun's heat; they refresh them, and cause them "to bring forth and bud;" so shall the dew of God's favour descend upon his people, causing them again to live and flourish.

"The earth shall cast out the dead." The earth contributes to the revival of the plants which seemed to lie dead in it,—it casts them forth. And in like manner, not merely the dew of heaven, but the fatness of earth also will not be awanting in doing its part when the Church with its interests is restored.

But there is, it may be, an allusion also to that which is closely connected with the restoration of God's ancient people; along with their revival the fulness of the Gentiles shall come in, and the promise of the text will be remarkably fulfilled when Antichrist shall be overthrown—when Babylon shall have fallen to rise no more—when Jew and Gentile, the whole family of mankind, shall be united in one glorious Church!

But, further, the text most unquestionably has reference to the final resurrection, and in particular to the resurrection of the saints. To this we now turn.

II. The doctrine set forth in the text. We do not say that this was what the prophet had *directly* in view, or what the Spirit of God designed in this passage particularly to set forth. The primary application of the passage we have already shown. But the employment of the resurrection of the body to illustrate the revival and triumphant progress of Christ's Church and people, is a proof that the doctrine of the resurrection was well established from the beginning, and fully understood as part of the creed of God's ancient people. Such illustration could not have been employed, had not the doctrine of the resurrection been known and accredited. In the creed of Abel, of Noah, of Job, of Abraham, of Moses, of David, of Isaiah, of all the prophets, as well as in the creed of the apostles, evangelists, and martyrs, the article of the resurrection had a place. The Jewish doctors, indeed, comparing the text with the sixteenth verse of the chapter, infer that only the Jews, only Abraham's posterity, shall rise; but our Lord tells us that "*all that are in their graves* shall hear the voice of the Son of man, and shall come forth; they that have done good, unto the resurrection of life; and they that have done evil, unto the resurrection of damnation."

Brethren, this doctrine of the resurrection and of the judgment is no new doctrine. Enoch, the seventh from Adam, prophesied of it: "Behold, the Lord cometh with ten thousand of his saints to execute judgment upon all." Job declared his belief and his hope in words which we have already quoted. Moses heard it proclaimed at the burning bush when God revealed himself as the God of Abraham, of Isaac, and of Jacob,—the God "not of the dead, but of the living." It appeared that the relation in which God stood to his people was a connection not dissolved by death. David thus expressed his faith and hope: "Thou wilt not leave my soul in the grave; neither wilt thou suffer thine Holy One to see corruption. Thou wilt show me the path of life: in thy presence is fulness of joy; at thy right hand there are pleasures for evermore." And again, "As for me I will behold thy face in righteousness: I shall be satisfied, when I awake with thy likeness."

Daniel prophesied thus: "Many of them that sleep in the dust of the earth shall awake, some to everlasting life, and some to shame and everlasting contempt. And they that be wise shall shine as the brightness of the firmament; and they that turn many to righteousness as the stars for ever and ever" (Dan. xii. 2, 3).

Our Lord brought "life and immortality to light," that is, he brought them into a light *more clear* and *full*. He brought the resurrection prominently forward, he illustrated and enforced it by parables, by promises and threatenings, by reference to former revelations, and by his own rising from the dead. The apostles taught the same doctrine, and proclaimed as a ground of undoubting confidence, that Christ had risen. He had risen and become "the first fruits of them that slept." We have reason to be cheered by the blessed hope of the gospel, "looking for the Saviour, the Lord Jesus Christ: who shall change the body of our humiliation, that it may be fashioned like unto his glorious body, according to the working whereby he is able even to subdue all things unto himself."

There were, indeed, those in the apostles' days who denied the doctrine, "who said that the resurrection was past already, and overthrew the faith of some." But those who were baptized and took their places in the Church, filling up the ranks instead of those who had fallen asleep, would not have known what to turn to for comfort and support had they been deprived of their hope of glory.[1] "If in this life only they had had hope, they would have been of all men most miserable." They had good hope through grace, and were sustained by it; the blessed prospect of Christ's glorious appearing filled them with peace and joy.

The answer Christ gave to those who so ignorantly and unbelievingly questioned him regarding the future state, was: "Ye do err, not knowing the Scriptures, nor the power of God." They erred concerning his *promise* to raise the dead, and his *power* to accomplish it; but their error was one rather of the *heart* than of the *head*—it was that of the Epicureans of old, who said, "Let us eat and drink, for tomorrow we die;" it was simply a preference of a portion here to a portion in eternity. See that ye adhere to the ancient faith delivered to the saints, "Why should it be thought a thing incredible that God should raise the dead?" The heathen, indeed, did not know the doctrine; the philosophers rejected it as impossible, or as contrary to their favourite idea that *matter* was the origin of evil, and that the only way to perfection was by getting free of matter. But the Bible tells us that our first parents were at first innocent both in body and soul; it reveals to us the second Adam who in the *body* was holy, harmless, and undefiled; and it declares that Christ's people, becoming members of his body, are sanctified

---

[1] Alluding to 1 Cor. xv. 29, 30, explained by some in this way.—ED.

in soul, body, and spirit, and will in their whole nature be glorified in due time. Further, the argument from reason—harmonizing well with the argument from Scripture—is very convincing, that, as the body is the instrument of the soul in good and in evil, and as man has two natures—material and spiritual—in one person, he will be rewarded or punished in both. When God is worshipped, it is not only with our understandings and hearts, it is also with our bodies—the outstretched hands, the uplifted eye, the bended knee, it is with our whole man, it is with our *bodies* and our spirits, which are God's. And so, on the other hand, God is dishonoured both with the proud mind and rebellious heart, and with the *lying tongue*, the *lips profane*, the *hands unclean*, the *evil eye*, the *body defiled*. We thus see a foundation laid for the doctrine of the resurrection, and of the judgment to come, in the fact that body and soul are both concerned and employed in the service, or on the contrary, in the warfare with him. It is in the Bible, however, especially in the New Testament, that the doctrine is established. The Messiah here speaks: "Thy dead men shall live, together with *my* dead body shall they arise." These words seem to express the relationship betwixt Christ and his mystical body. Christ is the head, his people are the members of his body. The singular and plural, it is remarked by critics, are here united; the whole Church is considered as one body, and yet termed many: "*they* shall arise." The dew here mentioned, and compared to "the dew of herbs," is the dew of the Saviour's power and grace producing a rich herbage, and promising an abundant harvest. "Thy people," it is said (Ps. cx. 3.) "shall be willing in the day of thy power. From the womb of the morning thou hast the dew of thy youth." The believer, with the apostle Paul, seeks more and more to know "the power of Christ's resurrection and the fellowship of his sufferings, and to be made conformable to his death;" "to know Christ, and to be found in him."

Such is a view of the doctrine set forth in the text, and now, in the third place, we are to consider—

III. Some of the instructions to be derived from this subject.

1st. As addressed to a Church in depression it is a comforting text. As the dew gets to the roots of the herbs, and causes them to spring up in freshness and beauty, so shall the influence of divine grace cause the plants and trees in the vineyard of the Lord to revive and flourish. To the sufferers in the cause of truth and for righteousness' sake, the text speaks a cheering word; it is equivalent to such New Testament declarations as these—"Blessed are they which are persecuted for righteousness' sake, for theirs is the kingdom of heaven"— "If we suffer, we shall also reign with him"—"Ye which have followed me in the regeneration, when the Son of man shall sit in the throne of his glory, ye also shall sit upon twelve thrones, judging the twelve tribes of Israel.

And every one that hath forsaken houses, or brethren, or sisters, or father, or mother, or wife, or children, or lands, for my name's sake, shall receive an hundred-fold, and shall inherit everlasting life."

2d. With reference to the resurrection from the dead, the text speaks comfort to those who are *in Christ*, for it says: "Ye shall rise and reign with your living head." It says to those now labouring and suffering in the body, "The time is at hand when ye shall obtain glorious deliverance; the grave will be only a bed of sweet repose, whence ye shall rise on the resurrection morn glorious and immortal." It seems in bold apostrophe to address the saints whose bodies are asleep beneath the sod: "Awake, and sing, ye that dwell in dust," for your period of deliverance draws nigh.

3d. It cannot but be evident how unspeakably important it is to be united to Christ. If you are united to Christ you will be partakers of the blessed resurrection of the just, through your life-giving Head. "When he who is your life shall appear, O believers, ye also shall appear with him in glory!" But, ah! if you are yet in Adam, the first and old covenant-head, what shall we say *to* you or *of* you? *Of* you we must just say, "If they believe not in Christ, they shall die in their sins!" And yet *to* you we say, "Awake thou that sleepest, and arise from the dead, and Christ shall give thee light." Sleep not on till death overtake you, as it has overtaken many—*many* in this place who gave no evidence of anything except that they were "in the flesh," who never so much as sought to please God, but followed after vanities and became vain! O dear friends! it is most affecting to think of the many who die without hope, at least without any good, well-grounded hope; concerning whom it may be said that heaven was not their aim! We have heard of persons getting fortunes which they never looked for; but remember that the rule in regard to the heavenly inheritance is "Strive!" "Strive to enter in at the strait gate." "The kingdom of heaven suffereth violence." "Oh, strive ye to enter in." Labour to enter into the heavenly Canaan, lest any of you fall after the example of ancient Israel. Beware, lest there be in you the *evil heart of unbelief, departing* from the living God. "Exhort one another daily while it is called today, and so much the more as ye see the day approaching."

My dear friends, the occasion of our meeting and the scene around us are indeed interesting and instructive. We are surrounded with the dust of forefathers and friends, we stand where many of you worshipped in former times, where often the memorials of our Redeemer were set forth, many a sermon preached, many a prayer uttered, many a song of Zion sung. "Our fathers, where are they and the prophets, do they live for ever?" Ah, no! These graves and monumental stones remind us that the people are but grass; that *ministers* are but *earthen vessels*.

The monumental stone on which our text is engraved was erected by one who in his day was distinguished in the work of the Lord by diligence, zeal, and success. He was ordained in 1713; it was not, however, till 1742 that his labours were, attended with such remarkable success. The "Narrative" tells of the great things done at that period, of the many born again under his ministrations, of the crowds which assembled and heard with earnest heart the word of life, and of the recurring communions occasioned by the intense desire to enjoy such refreshing seasons. The sermons and Narrative of Mr. Robe, together with the holy character he bore, render his memory peculiarly precious. For eighty-four years this good man has rested from his labours. Two other ministers have since laboured here and finished their ministry among you. Their testimony was the same, their doctrine the same, and we have no new doctrine to proclaim; we have still nothing to publish but Jesus Christ and him crucified. Oh, will you not embrace the faithful saying? Will you not *believe* the gospel? Dearly beloved friends, the time is at hand when that trumpet shall sound, when that sand-glass of time shall be emptied of its last grain, when these graves shall be opened and the dead raised, the bodies which sleep around us in this church-yard awaking to life, and coming forth to shame or honour— to woe or bliss. Oh, that the account we render when we stand before the throne may be one of joy!

Blessed Jesus, the resurrection and the life, thou who quickenest whom thou wilt by thy word and Spirit, quicken us! Draw us, and we will run after thee. Thy word to Lazarus was, "Come forth!" and he that was dead obeyed thy summons; wilt thou call the dead souls here to life—wilt thou cause them to arise and stand up a living army to thy praise? Oh, ere thou callest to judgment—ere thou callest by the trumpet-blast to the great white throne, bring poor, wretched, blind, naked sinners to fall down in humble, earnest prayer before thy throne of grace! "Awake, O arm of the Lord," as in the days of old! "Turn us, O Lord our God, and cause thy countenance to shine, and so we shall be saved!"

Dearly beloved friends, when we part in a church or in a market we cannot be sure of meeting there again; but in the place of graves it is most certain we shall all meet. Yet there is a separation,—ah, serious thought! Two congregations of the departed—*right* and *left*. "Depart, ye cursed," or "Come, ye blessed," will announce and fix our eternal state. Oh, to be numbered with the saints in glory everlasting—to find mercy of the Lord in that day!

SERMON II

PREACHED IN THE PARISH CHURCH OF
KILSYTH, ON TUESDAY, 23RD JULY 1839,
BY REV. WILLIAM C. BURNS[1]

———

Thy people shall be willing in the day of thy power.

—Ps. cx. 3.

THE will, my friends, is the ruling faculty in
the soul of man, and a man's character is very
much determined by the prevailing bent of
this power within him. It is the office, you know, of the
memory to recollect what is past; it is the office of the
fancy to plan and devise what is new; it is the office of

[1] See Chapter VIII. These notes only exhibit the substance of a
discourse which was greatly expanded and lightened up in the
delivery. They may, however, serve to illustrate the *kind* of instruction,
so far as the substance is concerned, on which the revival movement
of that day might be said to rest.

the understanding to deliberate, of the conscience to pronounce the law of right and wrong, of the desires and affections to draw and impel, and above all these, the will sits, as it were, supreme, pronouncing the final decision, and thus determining what is to be done. If you get a man's will, you have him on your side, and may reckon on his support; whereas, though you may convince his understanding and delight his fancy, and move his affections, yet if his will remains opposed to you, he takes part against you. And thus, my friends, the state of the will is always made a matter of the first importance in inquiring into the position in which the soul of a man stands with regard to God. It is the crowning part of man's depravity that his will is opposed to the will of God; that he does that which God forbids, and leaves undone that which God commands. Jehovah says, "Thou shalt;" man impiously answers in his practice, if not in words, "I will not." Jehovah says, "Thou shalt not;" man again replies, "I will," thus seeking to be independent of Jehovah—to be as God, giving law to himself, and following his own will, instead of receiving the holy law of his Creator and making it the guide of all his resolutions. This is the state of the fallen soul by nature; and therefore, my friends, when God brings back in his infinite love the souls of his elect people to his service, he makes them willing. He has exalted, as you find from this Psalm, the Lord Jesus as mediator to the right hand of universal power; and while he promises to

Messiah that his enemies shall be made his footstool, he promises that those elect ones whom the Father gave him to redeem, and whom he purchased to himself with his own blood, shall be willing, inasmuch as when the will is once renewed and brought into the service of Jesus, the way is prepared for every other faculty being restored to holiness, and every thought being brought into captivity to the obedience of Christ.

In this promise two things, you perceive, require explanation: I. The nature of this willingness which Jehovah promises Christ's people shall have; and, II. The nature of that day of Jesus' power in which this is to be accomplished. In endeavouring to explain the former of these topics, I remark—

1st. Christ's people are willing to be saved by his imputed righteousness. This willingness appears to unconverted sinners as though it were not difficult to be attained; and many who are entirely unrenewed have the confidence that they possess it. They know that they are sinners, and being afraid, especially in times of distress and in the near prospect of death, of the wrath of a holy God, they most gladly cling to anything which affords them the prospect of safety, and thus, out of a mere desire for deliverance from hell, they would be very glad that the righteousness of Christ were accounted theirs, and that they should thus obtain forgiveness. This is in substance the kind of willingness for Christ's right-eousness that ungodly sinners possess, and not as if it were a saving appropriation of Jesus. But, my friends, though the faith of most persons who profess to follow Christ is little better than this universal desire for deliverance from pain produces, this is far different, indeed, from that willingness for Christ's imputed righteousness which his true people have. For observe, among other things, that in the willingness of the unconverted soul for Christ's righteousness there is no true and humbling conviction of personal unrighteousness. The sinner may see that God will accept nothing that he has done, and that he will charge him with the omission of thousands of duties, but then he does not feel nor acknowledge from the heart the propriety of God's doing so; he does not humbly pass sentence against himself according to the judgment of God, but proudly thinks, at least in his own breast, that there is no such heinousness in his sin as that it would be unworthy of God and a stain upon his holiness if he should be pardoned. And then again, though he may desire the benefit of Jesus' obedience, he has no true esteem for that obedience itself, he sees no glory in it, nor any such sufficiency in it that at the command of God he will venture his soul's eternity upon it and it alone; and so you always find that though such sinners profess that Christ is all their hope, they are unwilling to be convinced of their being great and flagrant sinners, and plainly discover that their chief trust is founded, not upon what Christ has done, but upon what they are themselves. On the contrary, when there is a true willingness to be saved by the imputed righteousness of Christ, the soul is truly convinced of sin, and feels assured that it cannot be saved by any efforts of its own, and that it were glorifying to God's holiness and justice to cast it for ever from his sight into the place of punishment; and then again, the soul, while it sees itself all vile, has obtained some discoveries of the glorious perfection of the work of Jesus, its superlative excellence in the sight of God, and rejoices in the thought of being allowed to rest on this for salvation, not only because it is sufficient to procure its deliverance from wrath, but because it also gloriously satisfies the demands of God's justice, and vindicates the honour of his holiness. But—

2d. Christ's people are willing to be brought into subjection to his kingly power. This is a still more clear and decisive mark of a true convert than the one which we have just been noticing. Those who desire Christ's righteousness merely from carnal motives, without any humbling knowledge of themselves, or any just esteem for its excellence, will always be found to shun the yoke of Christ. The end of their religion is peace; and if peace could be got without true conversion to the love of God, they would never seek after an attainment which is much too holy for their taste. In every heart, however, which Christ makes willing, there is a supreme desire to be brought under dominion to Christ's love, a holy hatred of all sin, and a real longing that Christ would come and set free the heart from every lust, and passion, and idol which oppose the law of God, and dispute the supreme place with him in its affections. It is true, as all real converts know, and as the Lord has so fully taught us by St. Paul, that the power of sin in the soul, though broken, is not destroyed, that the flesh warreth against the Spirit, and that not unfrequently the will, which is but partly renewed, seems to consent to sin. But even in such cases the man sins with a divided will; there is a secret wrestling against that desire which is for the time superior, and after a time the holy, spiritual will shows its supremacy, and the soul is humbled in deeper self-loathing and contrition in proportion to the degree in which it has backslidden from God. The soul of the true believer, though it is not free from sin, would be free entirely and for ever if a resolution of the will could give sin its death-blow. However, it is not so. Though the will be renewed, sin still dwells in the members. The believer would do good, and yet evil is present with him; he delights in the law of God after the inward man, and being unwillingly detained in bondage, he cries out with the apostle, "O wretched man that I am, who shall deliver me from the body of this death?" and willingly adds, rejoicing in Christ's kingly power to deliver him from sin, "I thank God through Jesus Christ my Lord." But—

3d. Christ's true people are willing to bear the cross in following him. It is one of the marks, you know, which Christ gives of the stony-ground hearers, that in times of persecution they fall away; but it is not so with Christ's true people. In giving themselves up to him they make no reserve, and are well satisfied to have him instead of all else that the world counts dear, and even at the expense of life itself. This last great sacrifice we are not at present called to make, but there are many others that still remain for God's people to try the reality of their attachment to Jesus, and the value which they set upon him. They are often called to confess his name before his enemies, and those who are his professed, but false-hearted friends; and many other trials they must endure, especially in the first days of their new life, when old companions observe the change of their character, and try every art, by means of smiles and frowns, and bribes and reproaches, to draw them back into their former ways; but in all such cases the true convert is willing to bear the cross. He finds it hard and painful, but easy in comparison to parting with Jesus. He naturally fears and shrinks from suffering, but by grace he still more fears and shrinks from sin, and if there is no alternative but either to deny his master or die for his name, he is enabled to be faithful still, yea, to rejoice that he is counted worthy to suffer shame for his holy and blessed name. We proceed now, however, in the second place, to remark regarding the day of Jesus' power here spoken of—

1st. This day is the time of his exaltation to the mediatorial throne. It is on this throne, you perceive, that in this Psalm he is spoken of as sitting as a priest and as a king; it is on this throne, at the right hand of the Majesty on high, that he wields the sceptre of universal dominion, and that he rules in the midst of his enemies on earth; and it is from this that he sends forth that power which makes his people willing to obey him. Jesus, you know, exercised his kingly power even before he came in the flesh and offered up that sacrifice on account of which the Father exalted him, and thus the saints under the Old Testament were brought in subjection to his law. But it is most properly after Christ ascended up on high that he received all power in heaven and on earth, and therefore the latter days, or the times which reach from his ascension to his second coming, are more properly called the day of his power, and it is in these, accordingly, that the great multitude of his redeemed are gathered under his sceptre. In these times, my friends, blessed be God, we are privileged to live, and are therefore called to look for the fulfilment of the glorious promises that relate to it and to it alone. But,—

2d. It is the day of Christ's power when the gospel is fully and freely preached. The gospel of Christ is called the *power* of God unto salvation to every one that believeth; to the Jew first, and also to the Greek. And it receives this grand appellation because it reveals Christ crucified, who, though he be to the Jews a stumbling-block, and to the Greeks foolishness, is yet to them that believe, both Jews and Greeks, Christ the power of God and the wisdom of God. And thus you see, my friends, that whenever the Lord intends to grant a day of his saving power to sinners, he raises up and sends forth ministers who determine with St. Paul to know nothing save Jesus Christ and him crucified. When God is frowning upon a people he does not always remove the public ordinances from among them, but withdrawing the teaching of his Spirit from those who come forward to preach his word, the pulpits become filled with men who know little or nothing of the power of God in their own hearts, and thus, though the preacher may study with diligence, and discuss with all the power of argument and learning and eloquence, that preaching of the cross, which is to them that perish foolishness, is wanting, the glories of Jesus' person and of Jesus' work, with all the rest of his unsearchable riches, are forgotten, or but slightly and seldom touched; and thus, though the minister may preach and the people hear from day to day, the power of God is awanting, and souls perish unconvinced and unconverted. When, however, the Lord in his mercy returns to a nation or a city to gather out of them a people for his name, he raises up ambassadors who know from personal experience the evil and the guilt of sin, and have been led by the Spirit to rejoice in Jesus as all their salvation and as all their desire, the chiefest among ten thousand, and altogether lovely. And then, my friends, the matchless glories of Emmanuel are displayed, his preciousness is opened up, his love to sinners, and his willingness to receive with the open arms of his infinite love all that feel their ruined condition and are anxious for deliverance, are proclaimed and magnified; and thus a day of grace from on high is introduced, sinners are awakened, and are drawn to receive the Lord Jesus, being made "willing in the day of his power." But,—

3d. This leads me to notice, in the last place, that the day of Christ's power is the time of the outpouring of his Spirit. The doctrine of Christ crucified is called the power of God, because it is the instrument which God employs in pulling down the strongholds of sin and Satan. But yet, my friends, this doctrine is, after all, but an instrument which cannot be effectual unless when it is wielded by the almighty Spirit of God, by whose divine agency it is alone that sinners are loosed from the bondage of Satan, and brought into the glorious liberty of God's children. Often is this great truth demonstrated in the experience of every Christian, and especially of every Christian minister. The truth of the gospel is often preached with clearness, fulness, earnestness, and affection, sinners are taught their ruined and perishing condition under the broken covenant of works, and Christ is freely held out to them and urgently pressed upon them, and yet they remain despisers and rejecters of the Lord from heaven, and the minister of Christ is often found in sadness to exclaim. Who hath believed our report, and to whom hath the arm of the Lord been revealed? The people hear, and are perhaps attentive, and begin to reform many of those sinful practices in which they formerly indulged, but yet their hearts remain unconvinced of sin, and unenlightened in the glorious knowledge of Christ, and unconverted to God, there is still little seeking of Christ in secret prayer, little alarm experienced on account of sin, and few serious efforts to receive the Lord Jesus, as he is freely offered. But oh, how changed is the scene when the Spirit is outpoured! Then the hearts of God's people become full to overflowing with love to Jesus, and are drawn forth in vehement desires, after his glorious appearing, to build up Zion. They are much in secret, and much in united prayer, and are cheered by the gladdening hope that the Lord is soon to listen to the groaning of the prisoner, and save those that are appointed unto death. The ministers of God, also, are in general particularly enlivened and refreshed in their own souls. In private they are deeply humbled in soul before the Lord, and have an uncommon measure of the Spirit of supplication for sinners given them, with ardent love to Christ, melting compassion for perishing souls, and vehement desires for their salvation; and then, when they come to preach Jesus, they are evidently anointed with the Holy Ghost and with power, they speak with holy unction, earnestness, and affection, and sometimes hardly know how to leave off beseeching sinners to be reconciled to God. And then observe the frame of the hearers at such a time. Formerly no terror could awaken them from their sleep of death, they still said. Peace and safety, though sudden destruction was coming upon them; but now a few words are enough to pierce their inmost heart, and make them cry out often aloud and against their will. Men and brethren, what shall we do? Formerly Jesus was held forth and was despised, but now every word that tells of his love is precious, his name is as ointment poured forth, and sinners are filled with an agony of desire for a saving union unto him. Men, and women, and children, retire from the house of God, not to profane the evening of God's day in idle talk or idle strolling. They have much business to do with God. Their doors are shut, their Bibles are in their hands, or they are crying to God upon their knees as they are conversing with the godly, and obtaining the benefit of their counsel to guide them on the way to Jesus. These, my friends, are, you know, some of the marks of a day of the power of Jesus. When the Spirit is poured out from on high, and sinners' hearts are moved, the iron sinews of their necks are relaxed, and their brows of brass are crowned with shame; they flock to take shelter under his wings, like doves to their windows; they rejoice in his love as men that divide the spoil. Satan is discomfited, his captives are set free, and God is glorified. Such times of refreshing as these have been often experienced, and are destined to be still more gloriously displayed in coming times. Pentecost—Reformation—in Scotland, England, Ireland, particularly in Scotland—Shotts—Ayr—Irvine—Cambuslang—Kilsyth—Moulin—Glenlyon—Arran, and Skye.

HEADS OF APPLICATION

1. We have cause to lament—few willing—little appearance of a day of power—but cause also for joy and thankfulness—we live under the Pentecost times, we have had the gospel fully preached—and the Spirit has been sending you a few drops to excite a desire for more of his power.

2. Sinners! will not ye come to Jesus?—accept of his righteousness—submit to his blessed power—why not?—what have you worth comparing with his love? &c.—come, come, come!

3. Christians! are you desiring a day of power?—some of you stand in God's way—ye do not want a day of power—it would make you live more holily—expose you to more reproach, &c.—oh, shame! shame!—sinners perishing—Jesus despised, and yet you do not want a day of power. Pray, pray, pray—secretly, unitedly, fervently, with faith and importunity—"The Lord's hand is *not* shortened that," &c.—examples of the power of prayer—Shotts, Cambuslang, Kilsyth—time short—soon prayers at an end—removed from the footstool—power will come—but not by us—we shall be ashamed to meet our Lord! to look sinners in the face at judgment! &c.

Conclusion extempore,—Σὺν θεῷ, τῷ πατρὶ κὰι ὑιῷ κὰι ἁγιῷ πνεύματι. Ὡ μονῷ θεῷ ἡ δόξα εἰς τοὺς αἰῶνάς. Ἀμήν.[1]

[1] [Greek: With God, the Father and the Son and the Holy Spirit, the only God be glory for ever. Amen.]

SERMON III

A faithful man who can find?—PROV. xx. 6.[1]

WHO is it that asks this question? Is it some disappointed, querulous recluse, who has taken a disgust at all his kind, who thus gives utterance to his uncharitable opinion of his fellow-creatures? No! It is the language of Solomon, the wise and the wealthy son and successor of David in the throne and kingdom of Israel and Judah. The question, brethren, is still applicable, and the character here sought for still rare. The conclusion come to by the same king in his Ecclesiastes, is, "Lo, this only have I found, that God made man upright, but they have sought out many inventions."

The first part of the verse says, that to proclaim one's own goodness, kindness, and beneficence is common. Vanity and ostentation are very prevailing sins and

---

[1] The Author's last sermon. See Chapter XI.

foibles of human nature, but real goodness—fulfilling and going beyond promises—is very rare. "A faithful man who can find?" And yet, such an one ought not to be rare, but of everyday occurrence. Were men, were Christian men what they should be, and profess to be, the faithful would be found without any search; we should meet them at every corner. The unfaithful should be the rare exception to the rule. Yet we fear it is not so. The Nathanaels, the Israelites indeed, the children of Abraham in whom is no guile, are precious jewels, and rare as they are precious.

We are about addressing a call and invitation to the saints and faithful in Christ Jesus, to come to the feast clothed with the wedding garment, and you are charged, and we also, to search out the old leaven, and so to keep this feast with the unleavened bread of sincerity and truth. Let us give earnest heed to this subject. We propose to speak—1st, of some of those things which pertain to faithfulness, and wherein the want of it appears; 2d, to inquire into the reasons why true faithfulness is confessedly so rare; and 3d, to point out the practical uses of the whole. May the Lord teach us the things which differ, and make us sincere and without offence until the day of Christ.

I. In explaining faithfulness formerly, from Rev. xi. 10, we remarked its near relationship to faith. The word, indeed, properly means full of faith. It is a comprehensive character, implying both the principles and the practice, the root and the fruit. Thus, Abraham justified by faith, is called faithful Abraham; so that when we seek for a faithful man, we are just looking out for a genuine, thorough-going believer, not a mere talker or speculative professor of religion. But, more particularly, we observe—1st, *That the faithful are found in earnest about first table duties.* They know the Lord, acknowledge him as Jehovah, the true God, and as their God, and worship and glorify him accordingly. Whereas, the unfaithful give not that glory to God which is due, but they give that worship and glory to other objects, or, it may be, in theory and words they acknowledge God, but with their hearts they deny him. Where, then, are the faithful who *do give unfeignedly* to the Lord the glory due, who reverence his great name, who believe his testimony, and hearken to his voice, who honour the Son of his love, whom he commands all to serve and to obey even as they honour the Father. Where are those who at once bend to the authority of God's law as supreme, and to his revealed will as always an end of all controversy? Where are those who, calling Jesus, Lord, do in every case what he says without reserve, and without holding any conference with flesh and blood? Where are the Christians in mind, in heart, in hands, in feet, in every act, as well as in tongue—Christians in practice as well as in profession, in deed as in truth, in a foul day as well as in a fair day, in evil report as in good, in the world as well as in the Church, in the closet and on the house top, at home and abroad, at the watering-place as well as among friends at home, the same where known as not known? I have heard of a man of some station, speaking lightly or even mincing an oath to suit his company, who among friends maintained all due decorum. Others have appeared saints in public who are tyrants at home, or very negligent guardians of those of their own family.

Alas! where is the consistency here? where is the faith-fulness here? Is not this to deny the faith, and to be worse than an infidel? For faithfulness, let us look to Saul of Tarsus, really converted, who trembling and astonished says, "Lord, what wilt thou have me to do?"—and this not merely under the strong impulse of first impressions, but whose after course was a constant living, not to himself, but to Him who died for him, and rose again; and to those true converts who "were turned from their idols *to serve the living God*, and wait for his Son from heaven, even Jesus, who delivers from the wrath to come."

2dly, *The faithful are known by second table duties also.* Their faith in God is shown by maintaining good works, which are profitable to men. Faithfulness, indeed, is generally understood as expressed and evidenced by the due performance of relative duties, as of justice, of truth-fulness, of mercy, of doing to others as we could wish to be done to us. Both to the bodies and souls of men we owe services of various kinds, which put fidelity to the test, especially those which have respect to the souls of others.

But where shall we find a faithful man watching over and warning even the nearest relative, as a child, or a sister, a brother, or parent, or friend? How common to speak censoriously of faults, instead of faithful reproof tenderly and seasonably administered! And when self comes in the way, how apt are we to be warped and turned aside from the plain road of duty, either in a smaller or greater degree. If parents were faithful, how could it be that there should arise so many careless, ungodly children, how so many Sabbath-breakers, so many swearers, so many wasteful, idle smokers, so many drunkards, so many foolish and vain talkers, among our youth? How could these things be were there faithful dealing and good example shown to them at home, according to solemn promise made at baptism? How is it that so many who have taken up house have no altar for God, no sound of prayer or praise in the dwelling, morning or evening, Sabbath or Saturday, but just because they have never seen it in their father's house, having not had an Abraham or Jacob for their father, but rather a profane Esau and some daughter of Heth for their parents? And how is it that carelessness and want of trustworthiness is so much complained of in servants, but just for want of faithful dealing and good example by the head of the house? Oh, how much the reverse of Abraham's character is to be found, of whom Jehovah thus testifies, "I know him that he will command his children and household, and they shall keep the way of the Lord!" Servants take very much the cut, as we say, of their master and mistress, so that you may almost know the character of the house for piety and hospitality, or the want of these, by the conduct and manners of the inmates and domestics of the family. No doubt there are many exceptions both ways. There have been saints in Nero's household, and there have been also wicked and slothful servants even in the family of the man after God's own heart. But generally it is otherwise, for LIKE draws to LIKE; and there can be no fellowship between light and darkness, between righteousness and unrighteousness. Thus Jacob (Gen. xxxv.) makes a clean sweep of idols from his house, and sets up an altar for God, who had visited him in the day of his distress. The wonder is that so good a man was so dilatory in making this reform. And further, how is it that among children of the family foolish talking, and even lying, and something beyond *yea and nay*, even oaths, or half oaths, are carried down even so long as the race lasts? Is it not the unfaithful rearing and training, or rather the want of training, and of serious and affectionate dealing, which fosters, instead of counteracting, the native corruption of the heart of the young, and which keeps always in force the numerous moral evils which afflict society. But in seeking for a faithful man we trace his course in the world. We go to the house of business, to the shop or market. We examine the articles furnished, and the terms on which they are disposed of—whether they are composed of the ingredients which they purport to contain, and what the amount of profit charged upon them to the consumer; and we may find that though there may be no false balances, and no poisonous mixture employed, there is extortion in the charge, a Jewish interest exacted. In short, the customs connected with many branches of trade make it difficult to find a truly faithful man among them. One may not be able to cast a stone at another, and yet the whole fraternity may be found wanting in the balances of justice and of the sanctuary. At a fair or market it becomes a question of difficulty. A faithful man who can find? The faithful truth-teller has been described as a simpleton—and why? Because he has a regard to conscience and the golden rule. But too many act like him (a courtier) who said that he could not afford to keep a conscience, in other words, preferring gain to faithfulness.

But 3dly, *When we come to self, surely we shall find the faithful.* However unjust to the claims of the Supreme, or to fellow-creatures, though God be denied or neighbours over-reached, men will not neglect themselves. Nay, is it not just from selfishness that the claims of others are so flagrantly set aside? My dear friends, although it be most true that no man hateth his own flesh, and that selfishness is strongly rooted in us, yet, nevertheless, it is too true that even here we have been often notoriously in fault, unfaithful even to ourselves. What can be more true than that most men cruelly neglect their own souls, and prove cruel, and unjust, and unmerciful to themselves. Even the body is often injured, its health impaired, and its beauty deformed by the abominations of excess in meats and drinks, especially the latter, through sinful customs learned from parents or elder brothers, or companions vying with each other who shall most swiftly and successfully deform the human countenance and frame so wonderfully made. And then as to the soul, the nobler part of our frame, originally fashioned after the divine image! Ah, how shamefully and sinfully is this immortal part neglected! How disproportionate is the care and anxiety for the world's wealth compared with that for the heavenly inheritance. Alas! the greater number seem to mind everything rather than the interests of their never-dying souls! Ah, how few are faithful and true to themselves in examining their state, in making sure of their safety, and in watching against sin, and in securing their eternal salvation! How unwilling to be put on their guard! How unwelcome a faithful friend or reprover; so that while you would thank the man who kindly told you when going out of the road, or warned you from a bad bargain, you would probably be indignant at the real friend who would arise and warn you for your soul's good, who would come between you and the precipice of eternal ruin, who would bring you out of the broad, and lead you into the narrow way! Surely, few are faithful to themselves. Surely, many hate their own souls and love death. How few, like David, in Ps. cxix. 26, or like Jonathan Edwards, in the words of his diary, "resolve to lay open all their ways of thought and of acts; also, their sins, sorrows, and circumstances every day, and in all respects to declare their ways to the Lord himself ingenuously and honestly." Alas! instead of this, how do we deceive ourselves, hiding our sins like Adam, concealing them even from our own consciences, or suppressing the rising up of the truth before our minds! In minute and little things how unfaithful!—and yet it is the "little foxes which spoil the vines," and "he that is unfaithful in the least, will be unfaithful in that which is much." And again, "Whosoever shall break one of the least of these commandments, and teach men so, shall be the least in the kingdom of heaven; but whosoever shall do and teach the same, shall be greatest in the kingdom of heaven." And again, "Except your righteousness exceed and excel that of the Scribes and Pharisees, ye shall in no case enter into the kingdom of heaven." In the affair of worldly interests, it is a kind of axiom that if we take care of the little the large will take care of itself. This applies here. "Buy the truth and sell it not," in any part of it. The very snuffers and tongs of the altar must be of pure gold, and holiness must be written upon every vessel, greater or smaller. So much for the lesser matters of the law. But, alas! brethren, is there not in the great concerns of the soul and of religion a sadly prevailing defect of lively, and just, and solid apprehension and appreciation?

In one word, let us look through the commandments one by one,—the ten, and the sum of them,—and, examining ourselves by that pure standard of truth and duty, which is the will of the Father of our Lord Jesus Christ, let us say how it stands with us in this matter? Oh, how many of us thus weighed in the balance must be found wanting! "A faithful man who shall find?"

II. Some of the causes why there are not more faithful,—why still the complaint of few such. 1st. Just because the complaint of the prophet is still applicable: "Who hath believed our report, and to whom is the arm of the Lord revealed." Who has faith, and the precious faith of God's elect? or anything beyond speculation, or mere assent, or general profession? The truth has never been valued and bought,—it is easily parted with, or partially relinquished, or parcelled out. All men have not faith. There can be no faithfulness without faith as its principle, its root, and its moving spring; and if faith be either wanting altogether, or weak, so also will it be as to faithfulness, which will be either totally or in part lacking in truth and sincerity. 2dly. Because many are unconverted. This is, indeed, just saying the same nearly, in another form. Every one who believeth is born of God; and "to as many as receive Christ, to them he gives power to become the sons of God, even to them that believe in his name, who are born, not of blood, nor of the will of the flesh, nor of the will of man, but of God." The true origin of evil with the many unsteady walkers and unfaithful stewards in the Lord's vineyard is, that they have never been truly in Christ, new creatures; but the old man is still alive, the corrupt nature unsubdued, and the enmity not slain; the seed is sown on the rock, and soon withers, and disappoints the husbandman's hope; the tree is not of a good kind, and so the fruit is not good. Be renewed in the spirit of your mind, and then faithfulness will be the result. Make the tree good, and the fruit will be also good. 3dly. Vanity and self-confident vaunting produces unfaithfulness and instability. The first part of the verse says, "Every man," that is, every natural man, "will proclaim his own goodness;" and then follow the words of the text as a contrast. There is much meaning in this collocation of the words, intimating that the two things are closely connected, namely, vain boasting and unfaithfulness. There is a close connection in more than one way. This vain and vaunting spirit shows a want of the grace of God, a want of the true faith of the new heart; and then, besides, to gratify this vain-glory, what will a person not do, however inconsistent with the claims of God or of our neighbour? What the man needs is the humble and contrite heart,—in fact, he needs conversion. 4thly. The double-minded man is unstable in all his ways. You cannot serve two masters. It is impossible that you can be faithful to your great Lord, and Master, and Friend, to whom you owe unfeigned homage, and to whom faithfulness implies so much, if you at the same time are trying to serve mammon, or any other idol. Christ's authority as supreme must be acknowledged and acted out, if you would be found faithful. But is it not too often the case, and with too many, that men's opinions are too much regarded, while the mind of Christ is not sought nor regarded, whereas his will should be our law, and end of all controversy; and so it will be and must be viewed by all the faithful. Again, 5thly, Selfishness in one form or other is a great cause of being unfaithful to God, and also to our neighbour,—a great cause of supplanting, or abridging, or setting aside occasionally the claims both of the first and the second table of the law. Love of ease, of reputation, or of worldly interest, or fear of suffering the loss of any of those things, weighs too much with many, causing them to sacrifice duty and conscience to avoid the dreaded evil to their name or means, and to secure some supposed present good, which oversets the balance and causes the golden rule to be infringed. Witness Balaam, a sublime, inspired prophet and eloquent orator, describing in glowing terms the honour and blessedness of God's service, yet, through love of the wages of unrighteousness, proving himself utterly destitute of grace, and while obeying the letter, subverting the spirit of God's laws, and ensnaring others into sin by his example. The desire to stand well in the world's esteem, and to escape the reproach of the cross, has, alas! led many in former times, and in our own day, to fail in the season of trial, and to show themselves unfaithful. 6thly. Another cause is evil example. One time-server, and one slothful and worldly-minded professor of religion, infects another. This is a lamentation. "Many," says the apostle (Phil. iii. 18), "walk, of whom I have told you, and now even weeping, that they are the enemies of the cross of Christ." Observe they are many; one, and another, and another join company, and *like* draws to *like*. And, "because iniquity abounds, the love of many waxeth cold." Many are offended and walk no more with Christ—Will ye also go away? Yes, says the time-serving professor, I must go away; I cannot afford to keep a conscience so strictly and so constantly; I will not lay claim to a higher or firmer adherence to principle than such and such respectable characters, who have not relinquished their comfortable things, as some have done, at what they call the stern demand of duty. But, dearly beloved, be your reply to those who would thus seduce you from the straight road of integrity, and would have you give them countenance,—"Lord, to whom can we go? thou alone hast the words of eternal life, for whom we have suffered the loss of some things, and do count them as only dust under our feet in comparison of the knowledge of Christ Jesus, that we may win him and be found in him. 'Who shall separate us from the love of Christ?'" Lastly, the keeping judgment and eternity at a distance is a great cause of unfaithfulness. The day of reckoning is really near, but such is the influence of present things, and so obscurely seen as in the distance the final day of doom, that too many, Felix-like, say, when they have been somewhat impressed, "Go thy way for this time," &c.; and with the epicurean, "Tomorrow shall be as today." These, no doubt, are scarcely in point, if we view our subject strictly as referring to such as make a credible religious profession, but who are found wanting. Yet, in fact, it is just the same principle that is involved in both cases. It is truly wonderful, and it is melancholy to think, how slight and how small is the influence, even upon many professing Christians who say—as all do virtually, and some in the very daily language of their Church: "*We believe that thou shalt come to be our Judge,*"—how slight, I say, the impression of the vast eternity so near and certain, and of the great white throne of judgment, and of Him that sits upon it! Yet we must all appear before the judgment-seat of Christ; all! all! not one wanting, not one absent on that day! It is not left to option; we must appear. And the subject of examination on that day will just turn upon this of faithfulness. So we read in Matt. xxv., the sentence will be either—"Well done, good and faithful servant," or, "Depart from me, I know you not." Either, "Thou hast been faithful over a few things, I will make thee ruler over many things, enter into the joy of thy Lord;" or, "Wicked and slothful servant, who knewest thy Lord's will and didst it not, take thy part with hypocrites and unbelievers." And again, it is written in the gospel,—yea, they are the very words of our Lord Jesus Christ himself,—and they are very solemn, and fitted to make a deep impression upon each of us:

"Whoso shall deny me before men, him will I deny before my Father who is in heaven."

III. But this brings us at once to the conclusion of the whole subject. Having described unfaithfulness and the causes of its prevalence, let me shut up the discourse with a very few reflections. And, 1st, The subject presents ground for lamentation, that there are so few faithful, even among those who are Christ's professing people. Where might we expect to find the faithful, if not here?—yet it is said by our Lord, "When the Son of man cometh, shall he find faith in the earth?" How affecting to think of the state of the faithless, of their danger of losing their own souls, and of their ruining the souls of others, and of perpetuating and handing down the evil to posterity, instead of the fathers to the children declaring God's truth,—and what reason have we to fear God's judgments on the Church and on the land! The increase of corruption arising from unfaithfulness must sooner or later bring on judgments. "And I sought for a man among them that should make up the hedge, and stand in the gap before me for the land, that I should not destroy it; but I found none. Therefore have I poured out my indignation upon them; I have consumed them with the fire of my wrath: their own way have I recompensed upon their heads, saith the Lord God" (Ezek. xxii. 30, 31). How lamentable that even among leaders, who should be an example, there are so few faithful; and how is it to be lamented further, that party spirit and mean jealousies should divide those whose professed principles and general objects are the same, and should lead some actually to make common cause with the enemies of spiritual religion. What an unseemly condition! How unlike faithful men and followers of the Lamb! 2d. Be thankful that, though there be few, yet there are some faithful witnesses—a precious remnant, faithful among many faithless,—some standing up for good principles,—raising up, as from the dead, the truths which were in danger of being buried; bringing back, as it were, the spirit of the martyrs of former days, and giving Him all the glory. Let us, I say, bless God for these things, and yet further pray, "Arise, O Lord, and plead thine own cause." 3d. Let the faithful be encouraged, and learn their duty to continue faithful, and not to be shaken in mind nor troubled, though their number be few, for the foundation of God standeth sure. Truth loses not its value, yea, it rather rises in value and brightness when many oppose it. "Men make void thy law," says the Psalmist; what then? He only loves it the more. "Therefore I love thy commandments above gold, yea, above fine gold. Therefore I esteem all thy precepts concerning all things to be right; and I hate every false way" (Ps. cxix. 127, 128). The fewer the faithful, the greater the honour of being one of them; a few even in Sardis (Rev. iii. 4). 4th. Consider further, the manifold and inspiring motives to faithfulness. Consider who He is you are required to be faithful to,—even the glorious Jehovah, Lord of all. Consider the precious nature of the truths and laws with regard to which faithfulness is to be exercised. Consider your infinite obligations to Him who loved you, and, having redeemed you with his blood, called you to be his witnesses and his soldiers on earth. Consider the example of our Lord and Saviour himself, together with the great cloud of witnesses, the faithful of former days, who have finished their course with joy, and follow their bright example. Consider the many privileges you enjoy, the satisfaction of mind in being found faithful, and in the path of duty, the promises of God to faithfulness, and the provisions of the covenant to ensure your faithfulness. Consider, finally, the glorious prospects held out to you, the nearness of the period of deliverance from the evil reproach and suffering which may be incurred by faithfulness, and the bright crown of glory in prospect for those who stand faithful to the end. Consider these things, and thus arm and fortify your souls for whatever true faithfulness to your Lord may either impose or entail. Oh, even though you should have tribulation ten days, or even ten years, what matters it if all is well at last? "Be thou faithful unto death, and I will give thee the crown of life." 5th. See also at once a motive and an encouragement for prayer; the motive: "Help, Lord; for the godly man ceaseth; for the faithful fail from among the children of men" (Ps. xii. 1); the encouragement: With Him is the residue of the Spirit:

He can raise up children to Abraham even of the stones, or of serpents, or from lions. Witness Saul of Tarsus. Pray unitedly (Mal. iii. 16) for the fulfilment of the promise, "Race unto race shall praise thy works, and show thy mighty deeds."

Let the faithful ones be very humble, because you are so easily shaken, and because you are only in a measure faithful. Even in His people there is much dross and much leaven to be purged out. Pray, "Lord, enter not into judgment with thy servant." Even Abraham failed in that very grace in which he excelled. None are completely perfect except the Lord Jesus Christ. Look to him as the author and finisher of your faith. Be jealous over yourselves. Be on your guard against evil. Remember Peter. Remember Lot's wife. Often present the prayer, "Increase our faith." "Follow not at any time the multitude to do evil," but, "seeing we also are compassed about with so great a cloud of witnesses, let us lay aside every weight, and the sin which doth so easily beset us, and let us run with patience the race that is set before us, looking unto Jesus, the author and finisher of our faith; who, for the joy that was set before him, endured the cross, despising the shame, and is set down at the right hand of the throne of God" (Heb. xii. 1, 2). Pray for much of the Spirit's blessed influence, that you may be strengthened with all might in the inner man to all patience and long-suffering with joyfulness. And now, "unto Him who is able to keep you from falling, and to present you faultless before the presence of his glory with exceeding joy,—to the only wise God our Saviour, be glory and majesty, dominion and power, both now and ever. Amen."

SERMON IV

Therefore thus saith the Lord God, Behold, I lay in Zion for a foundation a stone, a tried stone, a precious corner-stone, a sure foundation: he that believeth shall not make haste.—Isa. xxviii. 16; read this text with 1 Pet. ii. 6.

MEN and Brethren,—The important prospects before us are such, that it is high time to look about for some sure foundation upon which to build our happiness. The fabric to be erected must endure long, for our souls will last for ever; and their eagerness for happiness will continue vehement for ever. The fabric must rise high, for our capacities perpetually expand; and a low happiness will not be equal to them. The fabric must be strong, proof against all the storms that will rise upon us, and upon this guilty world. Losses, bereavements, sicknesses, and a thousand other calamities, may yet try us. Evils are now breaking *in*, like a flood, and we, and our earthly all, are in danger of being overwhelmed. Death will certainly attack us; and that must be a strong building indeed which the King of Terrors will not be able to demolish. Now, *now* is the time for you to provide. And where will you look? Whither will you turn? This earth and all its pleasures will prove but a quicksand in that day. Your friends and relations can then afford you no support. If they can but find refuge for themselves, *that* will be all. Therefore, bethink yourselves once more, where you shall find a rock on which you may build a happiness that will stand in that day.

Let me dwell a little upon the properties of the foundation laid in Zion.

1. *It is a stone—a stone firm and durable.* Everything else is sliding sand. Wealth will prove a shadow, pleasure a dream, our own righteousness a spider's web. If on these we rely, disappointment and shame must be inevitable. Nothing but Christ, nothing but Christ, can stably support our spiritual interests, and realize our expectations of happiness. And blessed be God! He is sufficient for this purpose. Is "a stone" firm and solid? so is Jesus Christ. His power is almighty, able to support the meanest of his people that build their hopes on him, and render them proof against all the attacks of earth and hell. His righteousness is infinitely perfect, equal to the highest demands of the divine law, and therefore a firm immovable ground of trust. We may safely venture the weight of our eternal all upon this rock. It will stand

for ever without giving way under the heaviest pressure, without being broken by the most violent shock. Let thousands and millions build upon this foundation, and they shall never be moved. Is "a stone" durable and lasting? so is "Jesus Christ—the same yesterday, today, and for ever." His righteousness is an everlasting righteousness, his strength an everlasting strength. He liveth for ever to make intercession for his people, and therefore he is able to save to the uttermost all that come unto God by him. The rocks may decay; the firm foundations, and majestic buildings of antiquity, are now lying in ruinous heaps. But here is a foundation for immortal souls—immortal as themselves; a foundation that now stands as firm under Abel, Noah, and Abraham, as the first moment they ventured their souls upon it; a foundation that will remain the same to all eternity. Therefore it deserves the next character given it, namely:—

2. *A tried stone.*—Jesus Christ has been tried in the capacity of a Saviour, by thousands upon thousands of wretched, ruined creatures, who have always found him perfectly able, and as perfectly willing to expiate the most enormous guilt, to deliver from the most inveterate corruption. Thousands and millions have built their hopes upon this stone, and it has never failed so much as one of them. Manasseh and Saul, that had been bloody persecutors; the woman that was a sinner, the penitent malefactor on the cross—and many *Jerusalem* sinners who cried out, "Crucify him! crucify him!" and

thousands more who were sinners of the most atrocious character—idolatrous, and lascivious, and covetous, have ventured upon this rock with all their load of sin, and have found it able to sustain them. This stone is the foundation of that living temple—the Church, which has been now building for nearly six thousand years. All the saints from Adam to the present day, both those on earth and those in heaven, are living stones built upon this foundation stone; it supports the weight of all. And this trial may encourage all others to build upon it, for it is sufficient to bear them all.

3. This is a *precious stone*, more precious than rubies, the pearl of great price. Precious with regard to the Divine dignity of his person, and the unequalled excellencies of his mediatorial offices. In these, and in all respects, fairer than the children of men—chiefest among ten thousand—and, to the awakened sinner or enlightened believer, altogether lovely! How precious are his atoning blood and meritorious righteousness to the guilty, self-condemned soul! How precious that eternal salvation which he imparts: and how precious the price he paid for it, "no corruptible things as silver and gold, but his own precious blood." In short, he is altogether precious.

4. This stone is a SURE FOUNDATION, such as no pressure can shake—equal, more than equal to every weight, even to sin, which is the heaviest load in the world; the Rock of Ages such as never has failed, and never will fail those humble penitents who cast their burden upon the Lord

the Redeemer—who roll all their guilt, and fix their whole hopes upon this immovable basis. The foundation is sure. "Behold!" says the Lord God, "behold, *I* lay in Zion for a foundation, a stone, a tried stone, a precious corner-stone, A SURE FOUNDATION."

5. This is a *corner-stone.* It not only sustains, but it also unites the building. "He is '*our* peace,' who hath made both one; in whom all the building fitly framed together, groweth up into an holy temple in the Lord; in whom ye (Gentiles) also are builded together for an habitation of God through the Spirit" (Eph. ii. 14). Materials for this temple are dug out of all the barren quarries of corrupt nature, are collected from thrones and cottages, from bond and free, from Jews and Gentiles, from Europe, Asia, Africa, and America, and united in this corner-stone—all harmoniously compacted into one regular magnificent temple, where the God of heaven delights to dwell.

Jesus Christ may also be called a corner-stone, to signify his peculiar importance in this spiritual building. Hence he is repeatedly called the chief corner-stone, and the head of the corner (Matt. vii. 10; Luke xx. 17; Ps. cxviii. 22, &c. &c.) We are built upon the foundation of the apostles and prophets, but Jesus Christ himself is the chief corner-stone. It is he that holds up and connects all. Apostles and prophets, and all depend upon him, and derive all from him. But for him they would have no existence, no commission—their righteousness, their strength, are nothing without him. On him all their doctrines hang, in him they all terminate, and from him they all derive their efficacy. Take away this corner-stone, and instantly the saints in heaven fall from their thrones, and the saints on earth, that are gradually rising in heaven, sink for ever. Take away this corner-stone, and this glorious living temple, that has been building for so many ages, breaks to pieces, and covers heaven and earth with its ruins. But this cannot be. The foundation of God standeth sure. The chief corner-stone of the Church can never be moved out of its place.

6. Let us further observe, that this stone is a foundation. "Other foundation," says an apostle, "*can* no man lay than that is laid, which is Jesus Christ." He must be at the foundation of all, or the building cannot stand. To join our own righteousness with *his*, in our justification, is to form a junction of solid stone with wood, hay, and stubble. To make our own merit the ground of our claim to his righteousness; to hope that God will save us, for Christ's sake, because we are so good as to deserve *some* favour for our own sakes—this is to lay a foundation of stone upon a quicksand. The stone would stand if put in the proper place, that is, at the bottom of all, but not when thus reversed and placed above the quicksand. This is the refuge of lies; the delusive hiding-place, which multitudes are building at all their lives, with a great deal of pains; and, alas! when they think they have provided for themselves a strong everlasting

mansion, suddenly they feel themselves swept away by the overwhelming torrent of Divine indignation.

Here, then, let us pause, and turn our attention to a question which, we trust, you have been anticipating,—*"Am I a living stone built upon this foundation?"* Are you not anxious to make this discovery *now*, while you have time? if you have made a mistake, to correct it by pulling down the old building, and beginning a new one on the right foundation? Have you no anxiety about this? O dear brethren! can you really continue thus careless about eternal things? Ah! then, a dreadful hurricane of Divine wrath is gathering, which will burst upon you and sweep you away, unless you shall be founded upon the Rock of Ages. Think of the words of the prophet, "Behold I lay in Zion for a foundation, a stone, a tried stone, a precious corner-stone, a sure foundation, he that believeth shall not make haste" (Isa. xxviii. 16, 17). Then it follows—"Judgment also will I lay to the line, and righteousness to the plummet; and the hail shall sweep away the refuge of lies, and the waters shall over-flow the hiding-place." Think of the terrible consequences if you betake yourselves to some "refuge of lies!"

Would you then wish to know whether you are built upon this sure foundation? If so, I shall willingly assist you to make the trial.

1. Have you ever seen the utter insufficiency of every *other* foundation, so as that you feel yourself shut up to the faith of the Lord Jesus as your righteousness?

2. Have you perceived and felt Christ to be precious to you, so that your building on Christ has been an act at once of necessity and of free choice?

3. Where is your habitual dependence? Is it upon Jesus Christ alone, or is it upon Him and something else?

4. Is the life you live a life of faith on the Son of God? "To whom *coming*, as to a living stone, you are built up a spiritual house, an holy priesthood, growing up unto an holy temple in the Lord."

But if not founded on Christ, you *shall*, you *must*, unavoidably perish. Build your hopes ever so high, the fabric will fall and bury you in its ruins. Nay, this only foundation will be the occasion of your more aggravated guilt, and more dreadful destruction. "Unto you, therefore, which believe, he is precious, but unto them which are disobedient, the same is the head of the corner, and a stone of stumbling, and a rock of offence." And shall not all these alarming considerations have weight with you, to persuade you to make him your only foundation?

"Behold! I lay in Zion," &c. It is the Lord himself who speaks. Behold! it is my own work; understand, and believe, and rejoice. Ye poor sinking souls, *behold!* with wonder and gratitude. Say not, "I must sink for ever under my load of guilt," but turn to Jesus with sinking Peter, and cry, "Lord, save me!" and he will bear you up.

Behold! ye joyful believers, who stand firm like Mount Zion. Here is the Rock that supports you. Thankfully acknowledge it, and point it out to others as the only ground of hope for perishing souls.

Behold! ye self-righteous Pharisees, the only rock on which it will be safe even for you to build, after all you have done. Your proud, self-confident virtue, your boasted morality, is but a loose tottering foundation.

"Behold! ye despisers, and wonder, and perish." To you this only foundation is like to prove a stone of stumbling and a rock of offence.

Behold! ye glorious angels—behold the firm foundation Divine love has laid for the salvation of guilty worms. It is as firm as that on which you stand. We have one note additional to yours, for the Lamb was slain for us! "The stone rejected of the builders is the head of the corner. This is the doing of the Lord, and it is wondrous in our eyes." "O give thanks to the Lord, for he is good, for his mercy endureth for ever."

————

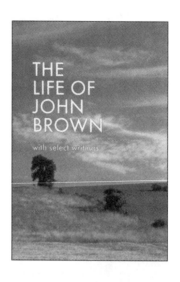

The Life of John Brown

William Brown

ISBN 978 1 85851 857 2 | 208pp. | clothbound

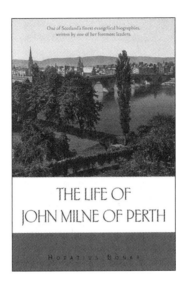

One of Scotland's finest evangelical biographies,
written by one of her foremost leaders.

THE LIFE OF
JOHN MILNE OF PERTH

HORATIUS BONAR

The Life of John Milne of Perth

Horatius Bonar

ISBN 978 0 85851 183 9 | 464pp. | clothbound

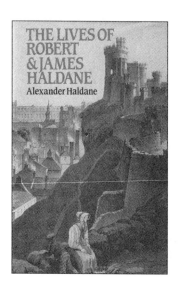

The Lives of
Robert & James Haldane

Alexander Haldane

ISBN 978 0 85851 567 0 | 728pp. | clothbound

Memoir & Remains of
Robert Murray M'Cheyne

Andrew Bonar

ISBN 978 0 85851 084 2 | 664pp. | clothbound

About the Publisher

The Banner of Truth Trust originated in 1957 in London. The founders believed that much of the best literature of historic Christianity had been allowed to fall into oblivion and that, under God, its recovery could well lead not only to a strengthening of the church, but to true revival.

Interdenominational in vision, this publishing work is now international, and our lists include a number of contemporary authors, together with classics from the past. The translation of these books into many languages is encouraged.

A monthly magazine, *The Banner of Truth,* is also published and further information about this, and all our other publications, may be found on our website or by contacting either of the offices below.

THE BANNER OF TRUTH TRUST

3 Murrayfield Road
Edinburgh, EH12 6EL
UK

P O Box 621, Carlisle
Pennsylvania 17013
USA

banneroftruth.org